The Ottomans

An Enthralling Overview of the Rise and Fall of the Ottoman Empire and the Life of Suleiman the Magnificent

Free limited time bonus

Stop for a moment. We have a free bonus set up for you. The problem is this: we forget 90% of everything that we read after 7 days. Crazy fact, right? Here's the solution: we've created a printable, 1-page pdf summary for this book that you're reading now. All you have to do to get your free pdf summary is to go to the following website:

https://livetolearn.lpages.co/enthrallinghistory/

Once you do, it will be intuitive. Enjoy, and thank you!

We forget 90% of everything that we've read in 7 days...

Get the free printable pdf summary of the book you've read AND much, much more... shhhh...

Enter Your Most Frequently Used Email to Get Started

DOWNLOAD FREE PDF SUMMARY

© Enthralling History

Table of Contents

Part 1: The Ottoman Empire

An Enthralling Guide to One of the Mightiest and Longest-Lasting Dynasties in World History

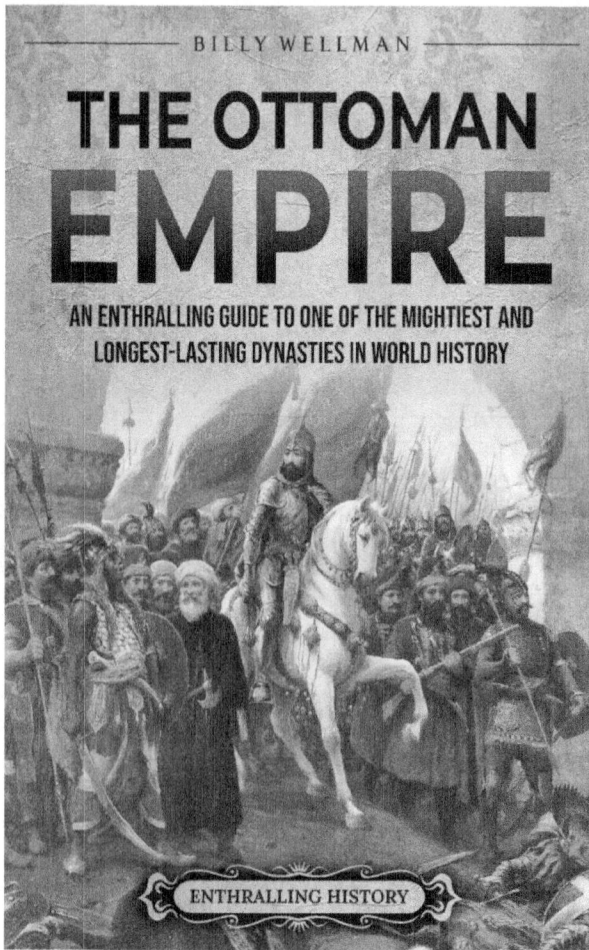

Introduction

The Ottoman Empire is undoubtedly one of the most interesting political entities that have emerged in world history. Rising from the ashes in Anatolia, a location where different kingdoms and cultures had clashed for dominance for centuries, the Ottomans quickly managed to subjugate their immediate neighbors and expand their empire far enough to include much of the modern-day Balkans, the North African coast, the Middle East, and Arabia. At its peak, the Ottoman Empire held immense power over its subjects and was feared for its excellent military, strong economy, and effective political system, which let the empire persist for over six centuries. The emergence of the Ottomans as a formidable European empire by the 16th century from just a small principality in the 1200s is a very intriguing phenomenon for historians to examine. And, of course, it is an interesting topic for curious readers of all ages and interests to explore as well.

But how exactly did the Ottomans manage to become so strong? What factors led to their rapid conquests, and what did the empire look like at the height of its power? And what caused its slow and painful decline and eventual dissolution after World War One? These are the questions this book will seek to answer. We will explore the history of the Ottoman Empire, starting from its deep and rather ambiguous roots in the Anatolian Peninsula to its collapse in the 20th century.

The first chapters of the book will cover the arrival of the Turkic nomadic peoples to Anatolia and their rise to power in a competitive environment against the mighty Byzantium. The opening chapters will briefly look at important events, such as the Battle of Manzikert, and conclude with the successful conquests of the Seljuk Turks and the formation of the Sultanate of Rum, which quickly became a daunting rival to the Byzantine Empire. Not only did the sultanate significantly weaken the Byzantines, upsetting the balance of power in the region, but it also served as sort of a predecessor to the Ottoman Empire, which was forged on the remnants of the sultanate.

The middle part of the book is concerned with the expansion of the Ottomans from a single principality to the most powerful actor in all of Anatolia. Here, we will explore some of the main figures that helped establish the Ottomans as a dominant player in regional politics and, thanks to continuous victories, contributed to various conquests against the Byzantine Empire, which was, by that time, counting its final days. By the 15th century, the Ottoman Empire's exponential expansion had caused the complete annihilation of the Byzantines, who were finally subjugated with the fall of Constantinople in 1453—one of the most significant events in world history. Against all odds, the Ottomans managed to defeat an ancient empire and truly become a force to be reckoned with. The Ottoman Empire even assumed the title of a caliphate—the most powerful Islamic state in the world—and spanned a vast territory, covering major parts of three continents.

However, these marvelous achievements would be followed by a small period of stagnation and reform, which required the Ottomans to confront many of the administrative problems innate to ruling a large and diverse empire. Instead of relying on external expansion, the Ottomans tried to consolidate power domestically.

Finally, the closing chapters of the book will touch upon the gradual decline the Ottoman Empire experienced from the late 18th century to World War One and its eventual collapse after the Treaty of Versailles. These chapters will take a closer look at the sociopolitical developments that made it difficult for the empire to make the advancements necessary to modernize, unlike most of its European counterparts. The wave of liberal nationalism that began after the French Revolution and swept through Europe turned out to be too difficult for the Ottomans to handle. Since the empire included people from many distinct ethnic, religious, and national backgrounds, it had to either give up its firm control over its subjects or instead tighten its grip and rule with an iron fist.

In the end, the Ottoman Empire was a victim of the pivotal revolutionary 19th century, a time when many other empires started their rapid demise because they were unable to keep up with their competitors. The book will close with the implications of the First World War and the creation of the Republic of Turkey, the main successor state of the Ottoman Empire.

Chapter 1: The Arrival of the Turks in Anatolia

This introductory chapter will cover the migration of the ancestors of the Ottoman Empire to the Anatolian Peninsula between the 8th and 10th centuries and the creation of the first Turkic states that challenged the Byzantine Empire. The arrival of the Turks in Anatolia was one of the most important demographic changes of the medieval era, producing outcomes that affected the world for many centuries. To better understand the early history of the Ottoman Empire, it is thus vital to have an idea of what was going on in the region before the Ottomans' rise to power.

First Signs of Turkification

The 14th-century Byzantine chronicles first used the term "Turkification," which describes the process of "becoming Turks." By then, the impact of the Turkic peoples on the Byzantine Empire and the rest of Asia Minor was clear. But who exactly are the Turkic peoples, and how did they arrive in Anatolia, where they established the foundation for the Ottoman Empire?

The exact origin of the Turks, just like many other peoples from Central and Northeast Asia, is unknown. Historians and anthropologists have speculated the Turkic peoples dwelt somewhere east of the Caspian Sea in the area known as the Transcaspian Steppes. They are thought to be relatives of the Hunnic tribes, which migrated westward starting from the 4th century and eventually reached Europe. The similarities between the Turks and the Huns are definitely there, ranging from their appearance to their spoken languages, but are perhaps most obvious when it comes to the structures of their societies. Peoples of Central and Northeast Asia lived nomadic lives, relying heavily on their horses, and were in constant movement, adopting agriculture later than other civilizations. Organized in strict hierarchical societies, they quickly became masters of equestrian warfare and dominated the neighboring lands, pillaging and looting everything on their way.

The Turks migrated in different waves from the Transcaspian Steppes, reaching not only the Middle East and eventually Anatolia but also settling north of the Caucasus in the open fields of modern-day central Russia. It is believed the scarcity of pastures and the heavy competition between local tribes caused them to start moving in masses to the west. After flocking to Iran, a strong confederation of Seljuk and Oghuz Turks defeated the local opposition they encountered and commenced the Turkification process of the Iranian people, which was not limited to just seizing territory. The Turks introduced thousands to their culture, customs, traditions, and language, effectively becoming a force to be reckoned with in northeastern Iran by the year 1040.

Under the leadership of Tughril, the Seljuk Turks quickly managed to overwhelm the Iranian people, thanks to their superior military, and subjugated the people of the region of Khorasan, the eastern plateau in Iran that served as a gateway between West and Central Asia. The Seljuks imposed tributes on those they conquered and controlled the trade routes that flowed through the region. The Seljuks gradually expanded, eventually reaching the city of Baghdad in 1055, where they defeated Arabs from the Abbasid Caliphate and converted to Islam. As the new sultan, Tughril swore to devote his life to attaining glory in the name of Islam and became committed to defending and expanding the Sunni Islamic faith.

The Seljuk Empire

Essentially replacing the Arabs as the most dominant Islamic peoples, the Seljuk Turks quickly emerged as a regional superpower and challenged their rivals for dominance. However, despite their military prowess, the empire would quickly show its flaws that were innate from its hierarchical tribal origins. After the death of Tughril in 1063, the Seljuks descended into chaos over the matter of succession, as the new sultan and different factions struggled for the throne for about a year. In the end, Tughril's nephew, Alp Arslan, managed to become the new sultan and ruled until the year 1072.

Alp Arslan led the Seljuks in multiple offensive wars, expanding the empire south and west of the Caspian Sea and reaching modern-day Armenia and Azerbaijan, which the Seljuks conquered easily. During his reign, the empire shared a border with the mighty Byzantine Empire, which was a direct threat and rival in the eyes of the Seljuks. The two sides clashed in small skirmishes many times, viewing each other as having hostile intentions, but the Turks triumphed in the decisive Battle of Manzikert in 1071, routing a much larger Byzantine army and capturing Emperor Romanus IV. Although the emperor would eventually be released after just one week of captivity, such a defeat to the Byzantines signaled the beginning of a long process of their demise and the emergence of new regional powers to take their place.

After the events of Manzikert, despite the fact that the two sides had agreed to a temporary truce, the Turks constantly raided the eastern Byzantine provinces. They were relentless, pillaging and burning small settlements and seizing loot and hundreds of people to sell as slaves. There was nothing the Byzantine Empire could do to stop them, as it lacked the necessary means to defeat the Seljuks in an open battle. The Turks, on the other hand, continued their expansion and became not only a problem in Anatolia but also reached the Holy Land and captured several big cities, including Jerusalem. Under Malik Shah, who succeeded Alp Arslan in 1072, the Seljuks invaded Georgia and unified all of Iran. It was a golden age for the Turks, as they made significant social and political advancements, including the opening of the university of Al-Nizamiyya in Baghdad.

The second half of the 11th century proved to be a magnificent time for the Seljuks, but in the end, it caused a well-overdue reaction from the west. Answering the call from the Byzantines, who had been plagued for decades by Turkish domination, and shocked by the fall of Jerusalem, Pope Urban II united the European Christians to launch the First Crusade in 1096, with the goal of liberating the Holy Land.

Sultanate of Rum

The reign of Malik Shah and his predecessors had been so successful that the Seljuk Empire was confronted with the problem of overextension. Despite recent developments, the structure of Turkish society was still not as advanced as European nations, meaning the governance of the newly acquired territories was increasingly difficult. This, when paired with a succession crisis that erupted after Malik Shah's death, caused the empire to divide into multiple smaller political entities. New rulers emerged in Syria, Iraq, Persia, and Anatolia, and although they were the descendants of the Seljuks, they started to operate separately, even choosing hostility over cooperation on multiple occasions.

Perhaps the most well-known state that was firmly established by the end of the 11th century was the Sultanate of Rum in Anatolia. The Seljuks in Anatolia had been largely autonomous from the center of the empire since the victory at Manzikert and had pursued the Turkification of Byzantine lands since the late 1070s. The name "Rum" was adopted from the Middle Persian term and referred to the Roman people who inhabited the lands of Asia Minor under the Byzantines.

The Sultanate of Rum, or the Sultanate of the Romans, quickly grew in power as a direct rival to the Byzantine Empire by the early 1100s. Due to the sultanate's increased efforts to undermine Byzantine rule and impose its own, the Europeans launched the First Crusade, trying to give much-needed help to the Byzantines in their fight against their Muslim foe.

The Sultanate of Rum is significant, at least in our case, because it is considered to be the predecessor of the Ottoman Empire, the latter of which later grew from a single principality after the dissolution of the Sultanate of Rum and the division of the Anatolian lands. However, for the first one hundred years of the Sultanate of Rum's existence, it dominated the Byzantine Empire and took over most of its eastern cities.

The capital of the sultanate was established at Iconium, right at its center, and beginning in the early 12th century, the sultanate expanded in all directions, eventually stretching its borders from the port city of Sinope on the Black Sea all the way to the

Mediterranean in the south.

Map of Anatolia and the Balkans in 1097.
https://commons.wikimedia.org/wiki/File:Anatoliabeforecrusade.svg

Continuing to fight in the name of Sunni Islam, in true Seljuk fashion, the Sultanate of Rum did not only bring Islam to the region but also set up the Muslim legal and administrative framework that would later be utilized by the Ottomans. The domination of the Anatolian lands and the control of the trading routes also allowed more and more Seljuks to migrate to the region, as its climate seemed more fit for their pastoral lifestyle. This wave of migration completely transformed the ethnic, religious, and linguistic structure of the region, diminishing the importance of Greek, which was widely spoken as the main language in much of the Hellenic world. Arabic and Persian were also prominent languages, but as the Turkish-speaking Ottomans replaced the ruling dynasty at the beginning of the 14th century, Turkish became the most used tongue.

Although the Sultanate of Rum greatly increased its territorial holdings, it was also the main protector of the Islamic people during the Crusades. The leaders of the Crusades always organized their routes to the Holy Land through the lands of Anatolia, which meant they often engaged with the Turks in battle to get to Jerusalem. Even though, initially, the Seljuks saw some victories, the sheer resources the Christian states poured into their expeditions rendered engagements almost useless. The Christian armies never seemed to stop, and the Turks quickly realized the disruption of their supply lines and hit-and-run tactics would be the best way to counter the invaders. The sultanate thus saw mixed success after a series of battles with the crusaders during the 12th century but nevertheless managed to retain most of its lands.

The sultanate's power slowly started to dwindle when succession wars weakened it. After the accession of the unpopular Kilij Arslan III, Ghiyath al-Din Kaykhusraw I seized control and divided the empire between his two sons. The 13th century brought a period of instability and chaos, as the rulers of the sultanate tried to further expand their lands but only saw partial success. They were repelled from their invasion of Georgia but acquired new territories on the southern coast of the Black Sea. The crusaders also contributed to the sultanate's demise, threatening its southern lands after having established a foothold in the Holy Land. However, the 13th century also saw the invasion of the Middle East and Asia Minor by the Mongols, who decimated all opposition on their way and subjugated the peoples of the lands they seized. After losing the pivotal city of Erzurum to the Mongols in 1242, Sultan Kaykhusraw II tried to retaliate a year later in the Battle of Kose Dag with the help of Christian mercenaries but was decisively defeated. He was then forced to accept to become a subject of the Mongols, failing to put an end to the chaotic political climate of Anatolia.

Despite the political struggles the sultanate experienced in the second half of its existence, its sociocultural role should not be understated. The Sultanate of Rum laid the foundations for the governance of Anatolia, which was later utilized by the Ottoman rulers. The Seljuk leaders massively improved the region's connectivity, setting up hundreds of trading posts and developing roads. Their methods of administration were also instrumental, as they took advantage of the many approaches in the region and introduced Persian and Arabic influences. Despite their differences, the Seljuks were quite tolerant toward the Greek people who inhabited Asia Minor, respecting their customs and traditions and incorporating Greek nobility into their own higher classes.

Chapter 2: Rise of the Ottomans

Having covered the origins of the Turkish people in Anatolia, it is time to move on to the main topic of this book. This chapter will cover the emergence of the Ottomans, first as a powerful principality and then as an empire. We will also talk about the political implications of the Sultanate of Rum's decline and how the Ottoman rulers utilized the opportunity.

Osman

After the Sultanate of Rum's defeat against the Mongol forces in 1243, the Seljuks in Anatolia became vassals of the Mongols, which ruled over the lands south of the western Middle East. The Mongols established a firm rule over their newly acquired subjects, granting them a degree of autonomy in return for tribute. However, the end of the 13th century and the beginning of the 14th century were a period of instability for the Mongols too. The sheer size of the Mongol dominion made it very difficult to effectively govern and control the people, especially considering the fact the Mongols had never been good at governance and administration in the first place. Slowly, the Mongol rulers started losing their grip over their Seljuk vassals in Anatolia, as different independent lords started gaining power.

With the increased migration of the Turks, the Byzantine Empire was also slowly weakening, but what really dealt a significant blow to the empire was the looting of Constantinople by the armies of the Fourth Crusade in 1261. The Latin Christians, who diverted from their original goal of capturing the Holy Land, instead sacked the city of Constantinople, further reducing the power of the already-weak Byzantine Empire. The Turkish principalities thus spawned farther and farther to the west, driving out the Greeks from the provinces they had historically occupied. Gradually, the Turks replaced the Byzantines in Anatolia.

Among the independent Turkish principalities that formed during the gradual decline of the Byzantine Empire was Osman's principality in northwestern Anatolia around the cities of Bursa, Nicomedia, and Nicaea. As the chronicle suggests, Osman was the first one in the dynasty to declare himself sovereign, and he managed to start the process of forming a new state. While waging a holy war (*ghaza*) against the Byzantine provinces with the goal of spreading Islam, Osman was able to attract the support of many neighboring principalities. They followed him into battle, presumably not only for the glory of Islam but also for their own material gain. Together, they launched a series of raids on the smaller Byzantine towns and villages, avoiding conflict with their Muslim neighbors in the south and east. Osman is considered to be the founder of the Ottoman state, which derives its name from its first ruler.

By the year 1300, Osman had maneuvered his way through the fragmented political climate of the region by securing alliances through a series of marriages and negotiations and consolidating his power in northwest Anatolia. Crucially, in 1301, Osman defeated a Byzantine army outside of the city of Nicomedia (Izmit), allowing him to gain control of the town of Yenisehir, which he declared the new capital, as well as access to the Aegean Sea to the west. By expanding westward, Osman was able to undermine the Byzantine rule in the region, essentially splitting the Byzantine territories into two separate areas. When Osman died in 1324, he had been dreaming of capturing the city of Bursa to really assert the dominance of the Ottoman state in western Anatolia and gain a significant advantage over its rival. Osman started the process, but Bursa wouldn't be taken until 1326.

Orhan and the Early Conquests

Osman's dream would be turned into reality by his son, Orhan, who inherited leadership of the state and managed to capture Bursa after a gruesome year-long siege in late 1326. Orhan declared Bursa the new capital and put in the effort to make it one of the most beautiful and prosperous cities in all of Anatolia. Most of our knowledge of Orhan's rule comes from the famous African traveler Ibn Battuta, who visited Bursa and other Ottoman towns in the mid-14th century. In his writings, Ibn Battuta describes the flourishing urban life, with rich bazaars surrounded by wide streets and pretty gardens. He also mentions the successes of Orhan's rule and praises him as a great warrior and administrator.

The Ottoman conquests continued with even more enthusiasm during Orhan's reign, who defeated Byzantine Emperor Andronikos III at the Battle of Pelecanum in 1329. The emperor was forced to flee after his forces were routed, freeing the way for Orhan to capture the city of Nicaea in 1331 and its bordering lands without much resistance. Pressured by not only the Ottomans but also the Serbian and Bulgarian leaders in the west, who had consolidated their forces to weaken the Byzantines, Emperor Andronikos reluctantly agreed to pay tribute to Orhan to stop the Ottoman threat while he focused on his problems in the Balkans.

Orhan continued to raid and pillage the Byzantine countryside before eventually capturing yet another important city, Nicomedia, in 1337. The merciful emir allowed the population of the city to peacefully evacuate to Constantinople before victoriously marching into it. With the capture of Nicomedia, the Ottomans became an undisputed force to be reckoned with in western Anatolia, and it was certainly the most powerful Seljuk principality (*beylik*).

Taking control of the key Byzantine port cities meant that Orhan had the means to launch further offensives in the west and push the Byzantines out of southern Thrace. After securing his eastern flank with other Seljuk rulers, he sent his son Suleyman to raid the shores of Greece. By 1354, the Ottomans had managed to significantly weaken the Byzantine coastal defenses, allowing for their first invasion of European territories held by Byzantium. With the capture of the strategically important Gallipoli Peninsula, Orhan was now in a prime position to challenge the Byzantine holdings in Thrace and the rest of the Balkans. The Byzantine Empire was now reduced to just a few isolated chunks of land that were disconnected from each other. Plagued by the constant Ottoman raids and the

Serbian independence war in the north, as well as Venice's increased influence on the seas and the unfortunate consequences of the Black Death, Byzantium's days were numbered. The Ottomans, on the other hand, had never been stronger.

Desperate times called for desperate measures, and Byzantine Emperor Cantacuzenus chose to ally with the Ottomans in return for military support against the Serbian uprising, which he believed was a more potent threat. It turned out to be a bittersweet decision. Orhan's son, Suleyman, successfully led the troops of the Greco-Turkish alliance against the Serbians when they invaded southern Thrace, but he refused to give up the advancements he had made, claiming he had been granted control of these territories by God. Suleyman was followed by the migrating Turkish settlers, who started dwelling in the Thracian lands, establishing Turkish settlements that would last for centuries.

Cantacuzenus was removed from power due to this fatal mistake, and the throne was seized by John V Palaiologos, who hoped to receive aid from western Europe to liberate the Ottoman-occupied territories. Europe, however, did not answer the call. The European nations were involved in wars with each other and had already spent a significant number of resources funding the disastrous Crusades. Thus, the European nations were reluctant to send help to the Byzantine emperor.

John V Palaiologos was fortunately able to find another, albeit temporary, solution to the problems of his realm. In early 1357, Suleyman, Orhan's eldest son and successor, tragically passed away, and the younger son of the Ottoman emir, Halil, was captured by local pirates. Since the Byzantines had a strong naval force, Orhan asked for the emperor's support to free his son from captivity, and the latter agreed, using the situation as an opportunity to cease hostilities between his realm and the Ottomans.

Emperor John V sent a rescue mission and was able to free the boy, but in return, he demanded Orhan put an end to the Ottoman conquests of Byzantine territories and wed his daughter, Princess Irene, to the young Halil, whom John had taken to Constantinople. It was a rather unpleasant agreement for Orhan, who was forced to accept it to guarantee his son's freedom.

Murad I and the Conquest of Thrace

Although the Byzantine Empire, or at least whatever was left of it, allied with the Ottomans, everyone knew the peace between the two was just temporary. After the agreement, Emperor John V once again tried to call upon the Western world for help but to no success. Upon Halil's release, Orhan broke the alliance and decided to launch another series of attacks on the remainder of the Byzantine lands, an expedition that looked to surround Constantinople from all sides. This time, the Ottoman forces, led by his second eldest son, Murad, crossed the border to enter Thrace with the objective of unifying the Thracian Ottoman holdings. It was another holy war, and it produced magnificent results for Orhan while decimating the Byzantine defenses. In late 1361, Prince Murad was able to besiege and capture the important city of Adrianople, proclaiming it the new capital of the Ottoman realm.

Prince Murad would become the Ottoman sultan in late 1362 after the death of Orhan. Just like his father and grandfather, his reign marked the continuation of expansionist policies and yielded amazing results. The capture of Adrianople, which was renamed Edirne, allowed Murad to push deeper into Thrace and consolidate whatever territories had been gained from previous invasions. Murad took his armies to Macedonia and Bulgaria, crushing the remnants of the Serbian uprising and subjugating the people who dwelled in these lands. Constantinople was effectively surrounded by Ottoman holdings or vassals of Murad. Turkish settlers quickly followed, establishing new centers in the captured territories and contributing to the process of Turkification.

However, before Murad could push farther into southeastern Europe, he was forced to return to Anatolia to deal with the principality of Karaman, which bordered the Ottomans in the east and had remained peaceful for many decades. Not only was Murad able to repel the enemy forces, but he also managed to conquer a large portion of land southeast of his realm, forcing peace with Karaman and signaling to other principalities that the Ottomans were the most powerful.

Murad I.

Murad returned back to Edirne to consolidate his forces. Having secured peace in the east, he was not ready to continue the conquest of the Balkans to choke out the Byzantines in Constantinople. However, once the Balkan nations saw the sultan abandon their frontiers, they united to put an end to Ottoman dominance. The Serbs assembled an army to resist Ottoman conquest, confronting Murad in the Battle of Maritsa near the village of Chernomen in modern-day Greece in September 1371. Although the exact account of the number of troops differs, it is believed the Serbian army outnumbered the Ottomans about nine to one, counting about fifty thousand men in total. Still, the Ottomans were able to outmaneuver the enemy due to superior tactics and gained a crucial victory that allowed them to continue the subjugation of the Balkans. In the following ten years, the Ottomans were able to capture important cities one by one, taking control of Sofia and Thessaloniki, for instance, by the mid-1380s.

Murad I completely dominated his enemies, even though he had to stretch his men over two fronts by the late 1380s. He had to deal yet again with the Turkish principalities in Anatolia, which had risen up to undermine the Ottomans' power in their home region. His successes produced a reactionary response in other Christian regions of the Balkans, leading to the creation of a coalition between the kingdoms of Serbia and Bosnia. Aided by the Knights Hospitaller, Prince Lazar of Serbia and King Tvrtko of Bosnia led about twenty thousand men against the Ottomans at the Battle of Plocnik in 1388, hoping that a Christian alliance would be enough to force the Muslim invaders back. Against all odds, the Christians managed to achieve victory, marking the first time they had defeated a large Ottoman force since the invasions of Suleyman a couple of decades back.

However, Murad retaliated, turning his attention from the east, where he had proven his dominance against the other Turkish principalities, and moving the bulk of the Ottoman army to the Balkans. Leading the men himself, Murad confronted the Christian alliance at the Battle of Kosovo in June 1389. Historians estimate that both armies counted around twenty-five thousand men. After a day of fierce fighting, both sides lost most of their troops, with neither one managing to gain a significant advantage over the other. Murad was killed during the fighting, but the Ottomans did not retreat; instead, they killed Prince Lazar of Serbia and pushed the enemy back. In the end, the outcome of the battle was inconclusive, with both commanders dead and the casualty toll similar. The Battle of Kosovo is remembered in Serbia today as a valiant effort on the part of the Orthodox Christians, who were trying to stop the Ottoman advance in Europe and buy time for the rest of the Christian European nations to react to the growing threat.

Despite Murad's death, the fighting spirit in the remainder of the Ottoman army and high command remained high. The Turks knew the alliance's manpower had been severely depleted. To them, it seemed impossible for the Christians to find enough strength for further resistance. The Ottoman army wanted more war and conquest, and a simple setback would not be enough to stop its drive. Murad's successor, Bayezid I, who proved his worth in the battle after the death of his father, became the new sultan and swore to continue the expansion of the realm. Nicknamed Yildirim ("Thunderbolt"), Bayezid I inspired his subjects due to his brave, chivalrous, and charismatic nature. He made the Serbs vassals, despite a close encounter on the fields of Kosovo soon after his accession. In 1390, to consolidate his Balkan possessions, he married Mileva Olivera, the daughter of Prince Lazar, and named Lazar's son as the sole ruler of Serbia, thus obtaining his loyalty to make sure that a Christian alliance would never again pose a problem for the Ottomans.

Defeating the Crusaders

Building on the efforts of his predecessors and pursuing an aggressive foreign policy, Bayezid I continued fighting the holy war in the name of Islam against the Christians of the Balkans but also made sure the Turkish principalities of Anatolia were aware of the Ottoman state's strength. He managed to take down and vassalize the leaders of the four western beyliks—the Karasids, Menteshe, Sarukhanids, and Aydinids—as well as conquer the lands of the Germiyanid principality, which lay in the heart of the peninsula, by early 1391. Two years later, after replenishing his forces and consolidating his power over his subjects, Sultan Bayezid I led his men back into the Balkans and took the fight to the Bulgarians, annexing their territories and completely surrounding the rest of the Byzantine Empire in a small isolated enclave at Constantinople. By 1395, Bayezid had vassalized the rulers of northern Greece and Wallachia, essentially Turkifying all of the southern Balkans and further stressing the fact that the Ottomans had become a major regional power.

Bayezid I's conquests alarmed the rest of Christian Europe, and Pope Boniface IX called for a new crusade to stop Ottoman advances in Europe in early 1396. The word of the Ottoman Empire's strength had spread all around Europe, but those in the west were still reluctant to contribute to the crusade. England and France were still fighting their Hundred Years' War, and the Iberian rulers were in the middle of the Reconquista. Thus, the pope's call was answered by King Sigismund of Hungary and Croatia, whose realm directly bordered the newly acquired

Ottoman territories. Sigismund was a powerful monarch, eventually becoming the Holy Roman emperor and ruling over the majority of central and eastern Europe until his death in 1437.

The most help Sigismund got was from John I, son of the duke of Burgundy, who came to the king's aid with a couple of thousand men, affecting the morale of the Christians who were motivated enough to join the cause. Soon, thousands of independent knights from all over Christian Europe joined Sigismund's army. The exact number of crusaders is highly disputed, with different chronicles painting drastically different pictures. It is reasonable to assume the Crusading force amounted to somewhere between fifty thousand to ninety thousand men, which was still an impressive feat considering the state of Christian Europe at that time. In early 1396, the crusaders started their march down the Danube River with the goal of defeating the Ottomans and liberating the Byzantine capital from the Turkish blockade.

Meanwhile, Bayezid I had completely surrounded Constantinople and even laid siege to the city, constructing fortifications to allow for a slow and gruesome capture of the Byzantines' crown jewel. When the word of the crusade reached the sultan's ears, he split up his forces and prepared to meet the enemy in battle. The crusaders reached the city of Vidin in western Bulgaria, whose leader, Ivan Srastsimir, had been vassalized by the Ottomans. However, upon seeing the crusader army, Ivan gave up control of the city and gave the crusaders a relatively easy way into the heart of the Ottoman Balkan territories. King Sigismund and his men continued their march down the Danube, targeting the crucial city of Nicopolis and pillaging and raiding the lands on their way in true crusader fashion.

In the summer of 1396, the crusader army crossed the Danube and besieged the fortress. Nicopolis, located at a natural defensive position where the Danube joined with the river Olt, was very difficult to take in an all-out assault. Garrisoned with about a couple hundred Ottomans, the high stone walls that surrounded the city could only be overcome after a long bombardment, something that was well known by the inhabitants of Nicopolis, who were hopeful their sultan would arrive to aid in their defense.

With no siege equipment, low discipline, and high expectations, the crusaders encamped near the city on its southern side, reluctant to launch an assault on Nicopolis so unprepared. Instead, the Christian commanders sent out raiding parties and scouting cavalry units to make sure they had assumed a safe position. However, as they waited, the word of Bayezid's advance quickly reached the ears of the high command, which started preparing for battle in mid-September. After discussing the battle plans, King Sigismund found himself in disagreement with the rest of his officers regarding the positioning of his forces, something that had plagued almost every crusade due to the diversity of the leaders and soldiers who came from different countries.

On September 25th, 1396, Bayezid approached Nicopolis to relieve the siege and found the crusaders stationed between his army and the castle walls, preventing him from going near the city. After setting up horse traps in front of the main infantry line, Sigismund was confident he could hold off the Ottomans. After a short stand-off, the two forces proceeded to clash in battle, but despite the high hopes of the Christians, the Ottoman cavalry turned out to be much more difficult to deal with than planned. By navigating the traps and outflanking the enemy, Bayezid's quick vanguard was able to crush the crusaders from the sides while the main infantry advanced forward and engaged in hand-to-hand combat. Overwhelmed by the enemy and struggling due to the lack of communication, Sigismund's forces started a mass retreat, with the different contingents of the crusader army being routed one by one. It was another decisive victory for the Ottomans.

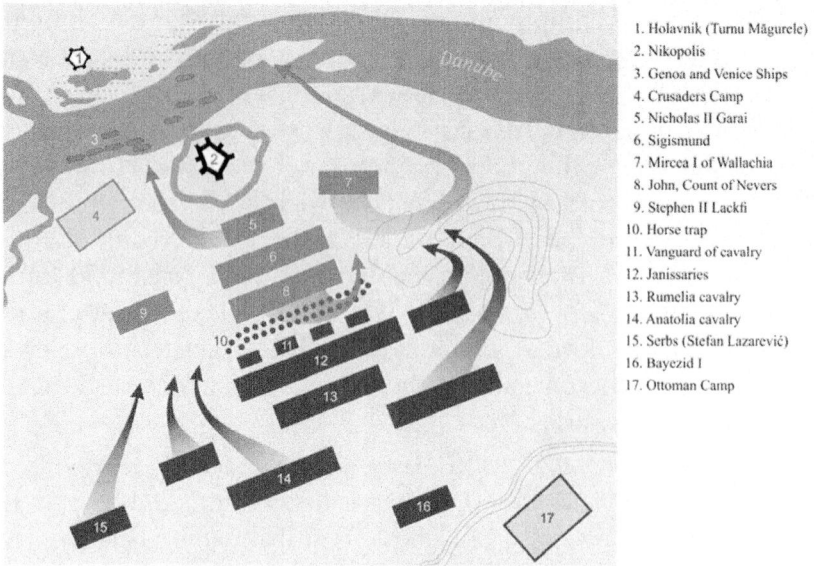

1. Holavnik (Turnu Măgurele)
2. Nikopolis
3. Genoa and Venice Ships
4. Crusaders Camp
5. Nicholas II Garai
6. Sigismund
7. Mircea I of Wallachia
8. John, Count of Nevers
9. Stephen II Lackfi
10. Horse trap
11. Vanguard of cavalry
12. Janissaries
13. Rumelia cavalry
14. Anatolia cavalry
15. Serbs (Stefan Lazarević)
16. Bayezid I
17. Ottoman Camp

Battle of Nicopolis.

Chapter 3: Challenges of the Empire

The previous chapter covered the rise of the Ottoman principality as the most dominant in Anatolia and the first hundred years of its existence as a regional power. Under its first few rulers, the Ottoman state managed to greatly expand its territories, waging not only holy wars against the Christians of Byzantium and the Balkans but also managing to undermine other Turkish principalities in Anatolia. With the victory against the crusaders at Nicopolis, the future looked promising for the Ottomans. However, as we will see in this chapter, the Ottomans would have to face a set of challenges and overcome external and domestic problems on their way to further expansion and domination.

Tamerlane

The Christian world was shocked by the defeat of Nicopolis. Europe had underestimated the true power of the Ottomans, as they had managed to quickly emerge as a true force to be reckoned with in the region. By the late 14th century, the Ottoman state covered most of western Anatolia, holding all the key coastal cities and almost all of the southern Balkans through direct ownership or vassals. The Byzantine Empire was at its weakest point, only controlling Constantinople and its immediate surroundings. The Christian nations had basically given up on another expedition to take back the lost territories, and the Anatolian principalities had largely accepted Ottoman suzerainty.

There was much discussion among the Ottoman high command regarding the future of the state after the Battle of Nicopolis. Although there were arguments for further expansion into Europe, Sultan Bayezid instead chose to return back to Asia Minor to consolidate his power. The sultan prized eastward conquests more than progress in the Balkans, viewing it as a gateway to the rich lands of the Outremer, which was dominated by the Arabs and the Egyptian Mamluks. However, this decision proved to be fatal for the sultan and forever affected his legacy. The main problem lay in the fact that the *gâzi* (commanders who waged holy wars), who comprised most of his army, were reluctant when it came to fighting other Muslims, whom they basically considered brothers. They were keener on waging holy wars in true Turkish fashion, just as their ancestors had done for centuries.

The Anatolian principalities, on the other hand, were quite familiar with what the Ottomans were capable of doing due to their disciplined army and vast resources. After Bayezid's endeavors in the Balkans, they had grown increasingly wary of the Ottomans and knew they needed good allies to resist if Bayezid decided to return east. However, the Ottomans had previously defeated a coalition of the principalities, meaning that coming together once again was not a guarantee they would be able to competently defend their lands. Thus, instead, they chose to rely on a newly emerged superpower, swearing their fealty in hopes that it would help them undermine Ottoman conquests.

This superpower was the Timurid Empire, a Turco-Mongolian state based on warfare and expansion that had managed to ruthlessly conquer the territories from western India and Central Asia all the way to eastern Anatolia, including key cities of Mesopotamia, like Baghdad and Mosul. It had even reached the Caucasus and subjugated the Kingdom of Georgia. The eastern Anatolian beyliks had already felt the might of the Timurids, led by the legendary Tamerlane, in the early 1390s after brutal raids and conquests had caused some of them to accept their superiority. After Tamerlane's return back to Asia Minor in 1399, the beyliks rallied once again behind the khan as their suzerain, believing the Ottomans were of no match to the Timurid forces.

Upon his return, Tamerlane sent an emissary to Sultan Bayezid, proposing that he swear fealty just like the other principalities had done and give up on taking over the rest of Anatolia. Instead of complying, Bayezid chose to answer with threats and demands of his own, which were at first disregarded by the khan. By early 1402, Tamerlane had established a firm presence in eastern Anatolia, reaching the city of Sivas, which he took from a ruler who was loyal to the Ottoman sultan. Tamerlane planned to head toward Ankara to consolidate his position.

Bayezid, with about eighty thousand troops, hurried to defend the city and stop the Timurid advance. His diverse army was composed of his *gâzi* and his Christian subjects from the Balkans. Bayezid met Tamerlane in battle in July 1402 near Ankara. Tamerlane had a superior army at his disposal and nearly twice as many men as Bayezid, including better cavalry regiments and, as some sources mention, even war elephants. Despite valiant fighting, the Ottomans suffered heavy losses and were decisively defeated. Bayezid was captured, and Ankara was taken by Tamerlane.

The Ottoman Civil War

The defeat at Ankara was disastrous for the Ottomans. With the sultan captured and the bulk of the army defeated by Tamerlane, the heart of the Ottoman state was open for the taking. The next decade would see the Ottomans descend into a period of chaos, uncertainty, and instability, where desperate measures would be taken to ensure the safety of the realm.

Surprisingly, Tamerlane treated Bayezid with respect, despite keeping him as his captive. Bayezid would die a year later in captivity, not long after Tamerlane's conquest of nearly all of Anatolia. Following his victory at Ankara, the Timurid khan managed to reach the Mediterranean and seized control of Izmir in December 1402. The Ottoman lords were unable to resist the Timurid raids, while the other beyliks had already sworn fealty to their Central Asian suzerain.

Although Tamerlane left Asia Minor shortly after his conquests and died in 1405, his plan for Asia Minor was to undermine Ottoman dominance by supporting smaller principalities and redistributing the power among them. He especially liked Mehmed, the *bey* of the Beylik of Karaman. Tamerlane gave him part of his own army and a fair share of former Ottoman territories to keep the peace and balance in the region before his departure.

As for the Ottomans, a civil war would break out among the four sons of Bayezid upon his death in 1403. The eldest son, Suleyman, was perhaps the most powerful out of the four, holding the capital city of Edirne and enjoying support not only from much of the *gâzi* but also from several Christian rulers with whom he had signed non-aggression pacts and truce treaties. For example, to gain financial aid from the Byzantines, he agreed to give back the city of Salonica in the autumn of 1403. Thus, after his father's death, Suleyman was the main contender to take the throne.

The second son of Bayezid, Isa, had established himself in the city of Bursa and hoped to assume power himself. However, he would be stopped in his tracks by Prince Mehmed, Bayezid's third son, who had accepted Timurid suzerainty at Amasya. In the battles that ensued, Mehmed and his supporters were able to defeat Isa's forces in mid-1403, forcing the latter to flee. Mehmed's men seized Bursa. Isa would later be murdered by Mehmed's agents in the Beylik of Karaman.

The two main camps were now established: Suleyman, with his supporters in the southern Balkans and Thrace, and Mehmed, who held the western Anatolian Ottoman holdings. Prince Suleyman was confident in his ability to defeat his brother and crossed the sea, capturing Bursa in March of 1404, not one year after Mehmed's victories against Isa. Chaos ensued among the Ottoman people, who did not know who to support. However, Suleyman did not just stop there, as he took his men to Ankara and captured the central city a couple of months after his victory at Bursa.

Following his conquests, a stalemate ensued between the two sides, which lasted for about five years. Mehmed's position was severely weakened, and it looked like Suleyman was going to triumph. However, the stalemate allowed Mehmed to rethink his strategy.

Before Suleyman's invasion, the fourth son of Bayezid, Musa, had been released by Tamerlane from captivity. Musa gathered enough support to fund his own expedition and suddenly attacked Suleyman's core provinces in Thrace, forcing the eldest brother to return from Anatolia. In Thrace, despite initial success, Suleyman would eventually be defeated by Musa at Edirne in 1411. Musa executed Suleyman, assuming the rulership of the territories previously held by him, and proceeded to lay siege on Constantinople, which had been Suleyman's close ally.

Desperate, Emperor Manuel II of the Byzantine Empire asked Mehmed to relieve the siege, promising him great concessions. Mehmed couldn't pass up such an opportunity, so he ventured to the Byzantine capital to save the Greeks from his brother, meeting him at the Battle of Çamurlu in modern-day Bulgaria in July 1413. It was a close battle, but Mehmed was able to defeat Musa, who fell on the battlefield. After the victory, Mehmed continued to reconquer the Thracian Ottoman territories to assert his rule over the subjects, cementing himself as the sole ruler of the Ottoman state by the end of the year. The Ottoman Civil War was finally over after about eleven years of constant infighting.

The first thing, naturally, on Sultan Mehmed I's agenda was to consolidate his power by assuring his subjects that he was the rightful ruler. After defeating his brother and retaking Thrace, he made sure to form a non-hostile relationship with the Byzantines. Although he had essentially saved Constantinople from Musa, Manuel II had supplied Mehmed with ships to transport his troops and equipment for battle, for which Mehmed I showed his gratitude. He returned the territories around Constantinople and the important city of Salonica to the emperor. Then, he proceeded to make peace with the European rulers, securing his western flank and signing non-aggression pacts with the Genoese and the Venetians, who were the most respected naval powers at the time.

It is important to highlight that the European Christians, who had been struggling with the Ottoman yoke for nearly a hundred years by the time the civil war broke out, were unable to seize the opportunity and fight for their freedom. Instead of rising up against the Ottomans, they largely remained relatively inactive during the decade of infighting between Bayezid's sons. Ultimately, this decision would prove to be fatal for them, as the Ottomans would continue to expand in Europe after the situation became more stable in the Ottoman Empire.

Having secured peace, Mehmed I turned his attention to his subjects, imprisoning or exiling those who had supported his brothers during the civil war and surrounding himself with men he trusted. After rebuilding his military, he chose to take the fight to the western Anatolian beyliks to restore the territories the Ottomans had lost during the conquests of Tamerlane. Although this campaign was rather successful, managing to take away valuable possessions from Karaman, a revolt in the European part of the realm caused the sultan to divert his attention westward.

Led by a mysterious religious figure by the name of Seyh Bedreddin, who had been previously exiled by Mehmed because of the influence he held over his supporters, the rebels rose up in Wallachia, denouncing the rulership of Mehmed in the name of their leader. Bedreddin was a rather controversial figure. A theologian, he had essentially led a sect of cult followers, challenging the principles of Islamic law. He was largely regarded as a dangerous radical. Hearing of his rebellion in Europe, Bedreddin's Anatolian supporters also rose up, further contributing to the chaos in the realm.

Mehmed's rule was also challenged by another mysterious figure who claimed to be the long-lost son of Sultan Bayezid, Prince Mustafa, who had been captured during the war with the Timurids by Tamerlane. "False Mustafa" managed to gain some military support from the Byzantines, who still wanted to weaken the Ottomans as much as possible in the hopes of regaining their lost territories. False Mustafa was also revered in other rebelling provinces in the European part of the Ottoman state.

Mehmed was forced to respond to the rebels, despite originally intending to launch an offensive on the beyliks. As a response, he sent two separate armies to deal with Bedreddin and False Mustafa, managing to crush the former in the autumn of 1416 and taking him as prisoner. In December, Mehmed publicly executed Seyh Bedreddin to show how any Ottoman man with rebellious and radical tendencies would be dealt with. False Mustafa was forced to flee to Constantinople, as his small force was quickly overpowered by the Ottoman army. After dealing with the rebels, Mehmed finally had time to conquer the remaining Anatolian beyliks. Before his death in 1421, he was able to take Hamid, Aydin, Menteşe, Teke, and Antalya, largely restoring the Ottoman borders to the ones during Bayezid's reign.

The Reign of Murad II

Mehmed I would be succeeded by his son, Murad II, whose reign can only be remembered as one of the most interesting in Ottoman history. The Ottomans would try to push further into Europe for the next two decades, something that produced mixed results due to the political maneuvering of the bordering Christian nations.

Interestingly, False Mustafa would play a dominant role in the first few years of Murad II's reign. The new sultan was confronted by the pretender soon after he ascended the throne, with the latter hoping to rise up before Murad could consolidate his power as sultan. This time, with Byzantine support, False Mustafa managed to take Edirne, but he was eventually defeated and executed at the Battle of Ulubad in early 1422.

Having dealt with False Mustafa, Murad wished to march on Constantinople to punish them for supporting the usurper. For many decades, Constantinople had remained as the Byzantine Empire's only holding amidst Ottoman lands, so taking the city would only be good news for the sultan. Unfortunately, however, before he could properly besiege the Byzantines, Murad was confronted by another set of rebellions, this time in Anatolian beyliks. The beys of Teke and Menteşe were swiftly dealt with, and by 1425, the sultan had regained control of the rebelling territories.

Murad II.
https://commons.wikimedia.org/wiki/File:Sultan_Gazi_Murad_Han_II_-_%D8%A7%D9%84%D8%B3%D9%84%D8%B7%D8%A7%D9%86_%D8%A7%D9%84%D8%BA%D8%A7%D8%B2%D9%8A_%D9%85%D8%B1%D8%A7%D8%AF_%D8%AE%D8%A7%D9%86_%D8%A7%D9%84%D8%AB%D8%A7%D9%86%D9%8A.jpg

For the next decade, the Ottomans tried to increase their presence in the Balkans, where they would mainly be challenged by two major actors: the Kingdom of Hungary and the Republic of Venice. Hungary, which lay just north of the Ottoman vassal states, was a Christian kingdom capable of putting up a good fight against the Muslims because of its military and economic power. On the other hand, the Venetians were the masters of the sea, dominating the trade in the Mediterranean and the Aegean and unwilling to give up their position of power.

Murad knew that he was not yet prepared for an all-out invasion of Hungary; it was rather large, and there was a good reason why no Ottoman ruler had dared to venture that far north. In addition, concentrating all of his forces in the Balkans would leave Anatolia exposed, and there was a strong possibility that another rebellion would break out, just as it had done countless times before. Thus, instead of an invasion, Murad organized a series of raids on the bordering Hungarian towns and countryside, with his soldiers raining devastation and destruction upon everything they encountered, which only served to weaken the Christians.

Hungary, however, viewed itself as the main defender of Christian Europe against the looming Ottoman threat and tried to influence the Christian Ottoman vassals of Wallachia and Serbia to join its cause. Although Wallachians and Serbians at first tried to resist the Ottoman yoke, they were rather reluctant to rise up in an open rebellion against their suzerains, fearing they would be crushed by the Muslims. Nevertheless, whenever Sultan Murad II directed his attention elsewhere, their nobles would declare their support to Hungary.

Eventually, in 1427, Murad signed a non-aggression treaty with Hungary for three years, with both sides recognizing the sovereignty of the new Serbian king, George Branković, and agreeing not to disrespect the organized borders. However, as one could easily imagine, the truce was doomed to fail from the beginning, as neither side had achieved their desired goals.

Throughout the 1430s, the Ottomans would constantly attack their Christian neighbors in the north, and the Christians would only retaliate once they believed their foe was weak. A good example of this is the Timurid invasion of Anatolia, which was led by Shah Rukh in 1435. By then, Murad had weakened the Christians with his raids but had to transfer his troops east to defend his positions. Eventually, the Ottoman sultan managed to get on relatively good terms with the shah, agreeing to give up influence over the central and western Anatolian beyliks and even helping the Timurids in their endeavors against the Egyptian Mamluks in the Outremer.

However, during this time, the sultan's influence in Thrace would significantly decrease, with the Christians enjoying a large degree of autonomy. Murad thus had to deal with them once again to ensure the safety of his realm. In late 1438 and early 1439, the Ottomans attacked and pillaged the towns of Christian Serbia, Bosnia, and Wallachia, managing to capture several important fortresses in the western Balkans. They even laid siege to Belgrade but failed to capture it.

Surprisingly, the response these military actions produced from Hungary was of the fiercest nature. The new king, Vladislav, with his fabled commander John Hunyadi, led forces over the border and confronted the Ottoman forces on several occasions throughout the early 1440s. In modern-day Romania, the Christians achieved a victory at the Battle of Hermannstadt in March 1422, routing about twenty thousand Ottoman troops and driving them back from Transylvania. After gaining the support of Serbia and Albania, John Hunyadi captured the town of Niš and further extended the tremendous momentum his army had managed to pick up.

In 1444, the Ottoman sultan was forced to sign a peace treaty with the Christians, as their rapid advances in Thrace were too much for the Ottoman forces to deal with. In June, the two parties met in Edirne. John Hunyadi demanded the Ottoman forces retreat from Europe and go back to Anatolia. Serbia was also restored as an independent state under George Branković. The Treaty of Edirne was one of the biggest losses the Ottomans faced in a long time.

Forced to abandon the defenses of his European holdings and with his military weaker than ever, Murad was left disappointed. He could not figure out a good way of governing his Christian subjects, who posed a threat to his ability to serve as sultan. Unfortunately for

Murad, he also had to sign a separate peace with the principality of Karaman in Anatolia, according to which he gave up even more territories in the east. The Ottoman state had lost its dominant position as a regional power, as it was unable to maintain control of conquered territories. Under heavy pressure from his subjects and after a series of military and political losses, Murad II abdicated the throne in 1444 in favor of his son Mehmed, who was only twelve years old.

Chapter 4: The Ottoman Empire

The first half of the 15th century did not exactly start well for the Ottoman state. Still recovering from the conquests of the Timurids under Tamerlane, the Ottomans were then divided for over a decade during the struggle for succession between Sultan Bayezid's sons. After the civil war, the country made some efforts to restore its former glory but was largely unsuccessful. Finally, the reign of Murad II was faced with multiple problems, as the Ottomans were once again pressured from the east and the west and were forced to give up more ground to their enemies.

However, as we will see in this chapter, the Ottomans would bounce back tremendously from their recent setbacks, starting a process of regional domination under Mehmed II that would last for a couple of hundred years. This chapter will cover the transformation of the Ottoman state into a true empire, a process that had immense sociopolitical implications for years to come.

Restoring Power

Murad's shocking decision to abdicate did not necessarily mean the country would overcome the difficulties it had faced over the last decade. Leaving the kingdom to a twelve-year-old only meant there would be new parties that would try to gain influence at the highest level. The power struggle that broke out after Murad's abdication, albeit not as violent as the civil war, evidently hurt the Crown more than helped it. What made matters worse was a new campaign organized by Hungary's King Vladislav against the

Ottomans, which was slowly approaching from the northwest. In a desperate situation, the Ottoman high command thus turned back to Murad, asking him to assume leadership of the armies.

This time, Vladislav's forces were far stronger and much more organized; they had even been blessed by the pope himself. Joined by contingents from Venice, Albania, and other European states and led, once again, by John Hunyadi, the new crusade organized itself in Buda and marched south, entering Bulgaria and defeating the local Ottoman garrisons in smaller towns. The aim of the Christians was to capture the Ottoman capital, Edirne, and liberate all Christian people who were forced to live under Muslim rule in the Balkans.

In November 1444, having been reinforced by local Bulgarian Christians, the crusaders marched upon the city of Varna in eastern Bulgaria. The strength of the Christian army is disputed, but estimates range anywhere from sixteen thousand to thirty thousand men. Nevertheless, the Ottoman force that confronted them at Varna was much larger, counting nearly sixty thousand troops, according to some chronicles.

Just like at Nicopolis about half a century earlier, the Ottomans arrived to relieve the city, sandwiching the Christians between them and the walls. On November 10th, the two sides engaged in fierce combat, with King Vladislav personally leading a cavalry charge against Murad, who was at the back with his royal guard. However, despite the Christians' valiant effort to break through the Ottoman line, the Muslim archers and superior infantry triumphed. Vladislav was killed in battle, and the Christians were routed. The Ottoman realm was safe once again.

Before his death in 1451, Murad II led the process of reunifying the lost Ottoman territories. Following his victory at Varna, he made sure to eliminate the enemies at his son's court, surrounding him with only those officials whom he personally knew and trusted. He quelled a small military uprising and set out to impose firm control over his vassals. In Europe, he eliminated local leaders and installed Ottoman rulers, thus bringing most of the southeastern Balkans under direct Ottoman rulership. Local princes were all replaced by Turkish administrators, as Murad realized that relying on foreign vassals posed a big threat to the empire's unity. By 1450, he also defended against another Hungarian invasion in Thrace and forced the pivotal province of Wallachia to accept Ottoman suzerainty.

In short, the final five years of Murad II's reign saw a series of rapid political transformations and the beginning of the process of building a true empire out of the Ottoman state.

The Capture of Constantinople

After Murad II's death in 1451, his son, Mehmed, now finally of age, became the new Ottoman sultan. Thanks to his father's tireless efforts, who, despite his military achievements, was never really into wars and preferred scholarship and a pacific lifestyle over conflict, the political climate was quite favorable for the new sultan. The borders of the realm had been restored to what they had been during the reign of Bayezid I, and there was relative stability in Anatolia and the Balkans.

The Ottomans were undoubtedly the strongest faction in the region, and for the first time in over five decades, the prospect of further expansion seemed realistic. The Timurids were getting weaker in the east, leaving the Turkish principalities potentially open for an invasion. In the northwest, the Hungarians had almost given up on attacking the Ottoman holdings, while the Christian vassals displayed no sign of rebellion.

However, Sultan Mehmed II chose neither of these traditional options for his first target. Instead, he had set his eyes on the crown jewel of civilization, Constantinople, which was still under the control of the Byzantine emperor. Constantinople was one of the richest and most important cities in all of the known world in the mid-15th century, and its enemies had tried multiple times over many generations to take it, with some seeing more success than others. Located right on the Bosphorus Strait, the city was strategically positioned, controlling the flow of trade between the Black Sea and the Mediterranean, something that had greatly contributed to its growth and had supplied the city for many centuries. Laying in the middle part of the lands controlled by the Ottomans, Constantinople had long been a logical target, but the sultans had never quite managed to get a hold of it, despite reducing the once-mighty Byzantine Empire into a pathetic political enclave.

Perhaps, most importantly, taking Constantinople would have huge symbolic implications in addition to the more obvious political and economic ones. It symbolized the "old glory" of the Roman Empire, something the Turks had previously emulated in the Sultanate of Rum when they saw themselves as the true successors of the Romans. Often referring to the city as Kizil Elma (the "Red Apple"), the Ottomans viewed Constantinople as their goal, a prized possession that would truly elevate the status of the Turkish state to the next level.

Constantinople's possessions in 1453.

Thus began a very tiresome and dutiful process of preparations to take the city. For nearly three years after Mehmed II's accession to the throne, the Ottomans mobilized all their strength and went through a rigorous procedure to soften up the city's defenses. Two fortresses were built on either side of the Bosphorus just a couple of miles away from Constantinople to oversee the total blockade of the city and destroy any ship that tried to break through it. Mehmed II diverted all his attention to the siege, slowly choking out Emperor Constantine XI Palaiologos inside the city walls by putting pressure from all sides. Ottoman forces were placed as patrols to defend the region from any relief forces that might have arrived from Christian Europe to save Constantinople.

The emperor wrote to Pope Nicholas V multiple times, asking to call a crusade to come to his aid, but the pope, who had no real influence over the Catholics at that time and due to the recent defeats of the Christians by Sultan Murad II, could not rally the

Christians. Over time, only about two thousand European troops arrived in Constantinople to reinforce the city, mostly coming from the Italian states of Venice and Genoa, which held colonies in the nearby islands of the Mediterranean, making the garrison about seven thousand strong, which was nothing compared to what the Ottomans were able to bring to the table. Constantine XI even tried sending emissaries to Sultan Mehmed, offering him to become his vassal and pay tribute to avoid the conflict, but the sultan responded by murdering the dignitaries, as he thought the Byzantine emperor's request was insulting.

Sultan Mehmed II.
https://commons.wikimedia.org/wiki/File:Fatih_Sultan_Mehmed_Han_-
_%D8%A7%D9%84%D8%B3%D9%84%D8%B7%D8%A7%D9%86_%D9%85%D8%AD
%D9%85%D8%AF_%D8%AE%D8%A7%D9%86_%D8%A7%D9%84%D9%81%D8%A7
%D8%AA%D8%AD.jpg

Finally, after years of preparation, Mehmed was ready to attack. To take the city, he assembled one of the mightiest Ottoman forces up until that point, counting no less than seventy thousand troops, most of them being of the highest quality. Crucially, the Ottoman force contained a significant contingent of artillery, new cannons, and bombards (large cannons) that operated on gunpowder and were beyond necessary during sieges. Sultan Mehmed personally oversaw the hiring of some of the military engineers who were able to build such weapons.

In April 1453, Mehmed II marched on the city and also sent his ships for a naval assault. Because the ships were unable to pass through the narrow, chained straits at the Golden Horn, just south of Constantinople, Mehmed ordered to take the ships out of the water and drag them overland to bypass the defenses and get to the city. All in all, it was a terrifying sight for the Byzantines, with hundreds trying to leave the city to escape their impending doom. Mehmed was closer than ever to taking the city; he had gotten further than any other sultan had.

Reaching the city in early April, the Ottomans started their bombardment, attempting to follow up the breaches in the walls with frontal assaults. These first attempts saw mixed success, as the Ottoman infantry was repelled by heavy archer fire, making it rather difficult to advance without suffering many casualties. Although the artillery softened up the walls, it was still the early days of cannons, so they needed a lot of time to reload, allowing the defenders to have time to mobilize their defenses. Then, the Ottoman army decided to build a network of tunnels to try and go under the tall stone walls of Constantinople, which surrounded the city and were nearly twenty kilometers (twelve miles) in total length. Unfortunately for the attackers, after weeks of planning and digging the tunnel system to gain access to the city, the Byzantines were able to get information about their plan after capturing some Ottoman officers, who were tortured and forced to reveal the army's plans.

Still, despite these setbacks, it was clear that, sooner or later, the Ottomans would simply overwhelm the Greeks due to their significant numerical advantage and higher-quality troops. In late May, after more than a month of back-and-forth, Mehmed II sent a letter to Constantine XI, demanding the emperor surrender the city. In return, Mehmed promised to let him and the inhabitants evacuate in peace. Constantine refused to give up control of the city but agreed to declare Mehmed as his suzerain and pay him heavy tribute annually. Although the emperor was hopeful this would convince the sultan, he practically signed his death warrant with his response.

The final assault on the city started on May 29th after three days of intense preparations by the Ottomans. Waves of Ottoman forces charged at the Byzantines and were able to rout the defenders at multiple chokepoints at the outer walls. After wounding the Genoise commander, the morale of the Ottomans skyrocketed while the Byzantines started to break. The attackers broke through, with thousands more following them inside the city. Emperor Constantine was killed during the fighting. Constantinople had fallen.

Mehmed II captures Constantinople, a painting by Jean-Joseph Benjamin-Constant.
https://commons.wikimedia.org/wiki/File:Benjamin-Constant-
The Entry of Mahomet II into Constantinople-1876.jpg)

The Ottoman forces had earned the right to pillage and raid, running rampant in the city for days. The sultan marched straight toward Hagia Sophia, perhaps the greatest Orthodox cathedral, and declared that it would be a mosque from then on. Then, he proclaimed Constantinople as his new capital, forever changing the Ottoman legacy.

On June 2nd, after three days of plunder, Mehmed ordered his armies to stop, seeing that the city had been reduced to ruins. He believed that a true emperor would never treat his subjects this mercilessly and pledged to rebuild Constantinople to its former glory. Soon enough, with the construction of new walls, mosques, ports, and bazaars, the city saw a period of great revival and continued to act as one of the centers of European civilization. As for the Greek population of the city, Mehmed showed the utmost tolerance toward them, allowing them to continue praying in the Orthodox churches. Many chronicles tell of the surprisingly kind nature with which Mehmed treated the conquered in the city, claiming that it was much more tolerant and much less violent than what the Christian crusaders had done in 1204. In Mehmed's eyes, he had inherited the noble throne of the Roman emperor, becoming the Fâtih, or the "Conqueror."

Ottoman Absolutism

The fall of Constantinople is undoubtedly one of the most impactful events of medieval history. It started a chain of political developments that rapidly transformed the world order of the 15th century and influenced the political process for many centuries in the future. Although most of the monarchs of western Europe had previously disregarded the potential threat of the Ottomans and were reluctant to acknowledge their true power, they were now forced to recognize that a new empire had assumed dominance in the region. In fact, the fall of Constantinople can be regarded as the start of the Ottoman "Golden Age" and the period from which the Turkish state emerged as a true empire.

As for Mehmed II, it was only the beginning. He was only twenty-one years old when he managed to achieve the feat that had been desired by the rulers who came before him. Thus, fresh from his magnificent victory, he would soon start working on increasing his power over his subjects to ensure total control of his empire. Mehmed II was one of the first Ottoman rulers who truly embraced absolutism as a way of ruling, distinguishing himself from everyone who was beneath him. He was to be the one and only person in the realm who made decisions, and anyone who dared to oppose him would meet a gruesome end, something he demonstrated many times throughout his reign. Mehmed built a new castle for himself in Constantinople, overlooking the Bosphorus and allowing him to be secluded from the rest of the officials beneath him. This was radically different from what the Ottoman sultans had done before; typically, they always were in the middle of decision-making on every matter and talked with their servants, commanders, and other officials.

Mehmed's conquests did not stop with Constantinople, as he was confronted, once again, with the matter of the Ottoman vassal states in the Balkans. Beginning in 1454, Mehmed became engaged in a series of conflicts with the Hungarians over the matter of Serbia, over which he planned to impose his influence. He failed to capture Belgrade in 1456, but a couple of years later, in 1459, he was able to defeat the Serbian opposition, directly occupying much of their lands.

After vassalizing Serbia, Mehmed II then turned his attention toward Venice, which had slowly emerged as one of the richest realms in Europe. Through its colonies, the Italian republic held a considerable chunk of land in Corinth and potentially posed a threat to Ottoman control in the region. Mehmed would never truly be able to undermine the influence of the Venetians in Greece, who continued to support their own people, thanks to their naval strength and fiercely defended fortresses in the area.

The Ottoman sultan found the most success in Bosnia, which he invaded in 1463 after confrontations with Venice proved ineffective. Despite the fact they were Orthodox Christians, Bosnians living in the Ottoman-occupied territories were quite open to conversion to Islam. This led to the construction of many mosques and Muslim schools in the cities, and Bosnian culture soon adopted Islamic elements, fusing them with its Slavic origins. The Bosnian nobility became close allies with the Ottomans and was often rewarded by different sultans for their integrity.

After Bosnia, Mehmed II faced his biggest challenge yet. In the early 1460s, eastern Anatolia had seen the emergence of a new Muslim ruler who gained so much power in the region that he established himself as a rival to Sultan Mehmed. His name was Uzun ("Tall") Hasan. Taking over as ruler of Aq Qoyunlu, a principality in southeast Anatolia, Uzun Hasan quickly defeated the bordering beyliks, eventually even achieving a victory against the Timurids and taking over the lands of Mesopotamia and Iran. By the time Mehmed had invaded Bosnia, Uzun Hasan's territories had stretched from the Persian Gulf all the way to the southern coast of the Black Sea, making him a natural rival to the Ottoman sultan.

The quick rise of Aq Qoyunlu was swiftly noticed by other Ottoman enemies, namely Hungary and Venice, which swiftly formed alliances with the Turkoman chief and supplied him with gold and weapons to wage war against the Ottomans. The invasion of the last of the independent Anatolian beyliks by Mehmed II ultimately triggered the conflict between the two sides. Between 1468 and 1470, the Ottoman sultan conquered Karaman and Dulkadir, which acted as a buffer between his realm and Aq Qoyunlu. Motivated by the Christians and the Karaman chiefs to wage war against Mehmed, Uzun Hasan mobilized his forces and declared war in 1472.

The plan was simple. Uzun Hasan would attack the Ottomans in Anatolia, liberating the annexed beyliks and closing in on Constantinople, while the Venetians would cause diversions in the western part of the empire with its navy. However, Mehmed II had long expected an invasion by Uzun Hasan and was able to muster up the experienced Ottoman army to its fullest extent. With the force of at least seventy thousand men, the two leaders confronted each other in northeastern Anatolia in August 1473. At the Battle of Otlukbeli, the Ottomans were able to effectively utilize their technological superiority, gunning down the enemy with the latest cannons, which had seen many upgrades since the siege of Constantinople.

With his army crushed, Uzun Hasan was forced to flee, but the Ottoman cavalry pursued the enemy for quite a long distance, eventually capturing thousands of prisoners after the battle. On the Ottomans' way back to Constantinople, now renamed Istanbul, Mehmed II executed hundreds of Aq Qoyunlu men in different cities of the Turkish beyliks, demonstrating the might of the Ottoman Empire once again to his subjects.

But the Ottoman sultan was not yet done when it came to conquests. Even though the Aq Qoyunlu Turks had been defeated, the Christian nations of Venice and Genoa, which had emerged as rivals of the Ottomans over the past decades, still had considerable influence in the region. Venice and Genoa were wealthy states. They were able to pay mercenary armies large sums of money to fight for them while also fielding the largest and the most powerful navies in the Mediterranean. They had not only colonized the islands of the Mediterranean but also had reached the Black Sea, organizing trading posts in Crimea, the Caucasus, and northern Anatolia and taking control of the valuable naval trade routes.

Aware of the threat they posed, Mehmed II launched a series of campaigns on the Italian colonies following his victory against Uzun Hasan. By late 1475, he had managed to capture the valuable cities of Sinop, Kaffa, and Trebizond from Genoa while also reducing the presence of Venice in the Balkans by taking parts of Albania and several islands in the Mediterranean. In exchange for peace and the right to pursue trade in the seas controlled by the Ottomans, the Italian states were forced to agree to pay annual tributes to the Ottoman sultan. Mehmed also offered protection to the Tatars who inhabited the Crimean Peninsula and were technically under the control of the Golden Horde. With Crimea on his side and Venice and Genoa weakened, the Ottoman sultan had effectively become the sole master of the naval trade in both the Black Sea and the eastern Mediterranean.

Mehmed II, also known as Mehmed the Conqueror, was an amazing Ottoman sultan who managed to elevate the realm to a completely different level. Of course, the capture of Constantinople is among his greatest achievements. But Mehmed II also made quite an effort to defend the empire from its enemies and extend its influence far beyond any other sultan before him. As perhaps the first absolutist ruler of the Ottoman Empire, he laid the foundations for the creation of a more modern, bureaucratic rule and helped the empire start its transformation from its old-fashioned, traditional roots to standards that were, by all means, European.

Valuing discipline and loyalty but also being open-minded and tolerant when need be, Mehmed II remains one of the most interesting figures in Ottoman history. Before his death in 1481, after nearly thirty years of ruling, Mehmed planned the invasion of Italy and had even established a base at Otranto to pursue his goals of reclaiming the glory once held by the Roman Empire. Who knows what would have happened if the sultan, who was still rather young, as he was only forty-nine years old, had lived to carry out his plans.

Bayezid II

After the death of Mehmed II, the Ottoman Empire found itself in a brief succession war between his two eldest sons: Prince Cem and Prince Bayezid. At the time of the sultan's death, there had been no designated heir to continue the succession, complicating the situation. Thus, several powerful political figures gained the support of the Janissary army corps stationed in Istanbul and killed Grand Vizier Mehmed Pasha, who had served as Mehmed II's right hand and favored the accession of Prince Cem to the throne. This allowed Prince Bayezid to declare himself the new sultan, while Prince Cem was forced to gather his supporters in the city of Bursa. There, Prince Cem proclaimed that he was the rightful heir to the throne and proposed that he and his brother divide the empire in two, with Cem becoming the ruler of Anatolia and Bayezid ruling over the western part of the Ottoman lands. Of course, this was not tolerated by Bayezid, who rallied his armies and confronted his brother near the town of Yenişehir, where he defeated Cem and ended the dispute, or at least so he thought.

Prince Cem and several of his powerful supporters managed to escape the battle, fleeing to the Mamluk territories to seek political refuge. There, the Mamluks provided the young prince with an army sufficient enough to pose a threat to Bayezid's claim. The Mamluks realized that a succession dispute in the Ottoman Empire meant a weaker rival and sought to exploit the situation as much as they could. With renewed spirit, in 1482, Prince Cem marched into Anatolia from Syria, joined by some local beys who had been stripped of their titles by Mehmed during his conquests and held grudges against the sultan. Promising to restore their independence and freedom in exchange for military support, Cem further promoted an all-out rebellion of the Turkish nobility against Bayezid and saw his numbers grow as he approached his brother.

However, despite his best efforts and even with the support of the Mamluks and the Turkish aristocracy, Cem's army was defeated on multiple occasions by Bayezid, most importantly at the city of Konya in the summer of 1482. Now hopeless, Prince Cem was forced to flee to the island of Rhodes, then occupied by the Knights Hospitaller, fearful that his brother would have him executed for treason.

Thus, Bayezid II became the sole sultan of the Ottoman Empire and, until his death in 1512, managed to strengthen the realm that had been left to him by his father. That is not to say that his reign did not see any wars. On the contrary, since early 1484, Bayezid saw himself engaged in a conflict with the Mamluks, who were now the

Ottoman Empire's main rival. The war lasted until 1491, the year the Mamluks sued for peace to deal with their domestic problems. This meant that the Ottomans assumed, for the first time, almost total dominance of the Anatolian Peninsula.

Bayezid II also campaigned against the Europeans, defeating the Moldavians in the north and capturing the valuable fortresses of Kilia and Akkerman on the western coast of the Black Sea in 1485. This further increased the power of the Ottomans in the region, allowing the sultan to push for further expansion in eastern Europe. The Ottoman Empire became engulfed in a long war with the Kingdom of Poland, which lasted until 1498. The Polish tried many times to launch successful offensives on the Turkish Moldavian holdings but were finally defeated in 1497 in the Battle of the Cosmin Forest, forcing them to accept peace.

Bayezid waged war against the Republic of Venice in 1499. He was finally able to reduce the Italian influence in Greece by capturing valuable castles in Modon, Lepanto, Koroni, and Navarino. In 1503, the Venetians were forced to sign a peace agreement, which forced them to give up much of their colonies in the eastern Mediterranean. The Ottomans thus controlled the trade flow from the Black Sea to the Mediterranean, and Turkish ports quickly grew in size and wealth following their sultan's successes.

Besides his wars, Sultan Bayezid II also improved the administrative system of the Ottoman Empire, again following in his father's footsteps. During his reign, the sultan made sure to surround himself with the men he personally trusted, despite their previous status in society or their family name. Old Turkish aristocrats were just as favored to occupy positions within the government as new faces that had appeared in court through the devshirme system, which recruited subjects fit for governance from the sultan's Balkan subjects. The devshirme system produced a considerable number of Turkified men of noble Christian descent, but Bayezid was the first sultan to utilize them effectively in his administration. By the end of his reign, not only were there many devshirme viziers occupying high-ranking positions, but they also acted as a balancing core to the Turkish nobility, which had largely enjoyed dominance before the implementation of the system.

In addition to giving more influence to the devshirme to achieve a better balance of his subjects, Bayezid II also introduced more liberal economic policies, especially after the success of his war with Venice greatly increased the flow of wealth into the empire. During Mehmed II's reign, taxes on all landowners were increased to support the war effort. Custom tariffs were high, and the coinage was devalued. Bayezid, on the other hand, lowered the taxes for the peasantry and redistributed the lands, giving them to those who had theirs stripped away from them in the past. Customs rates were also lowered to encourage foreign merchants to pass through Ottoman territories since the empire controlled the flow of trade in the region.

During the latter half of his reign, the sultan chose to pay less attention to the day-to-day administration of the empire, trusting his grand vizier with the matter. Instead, he spent more time in his palace, as he was keen on the arts and wished to grow his knowledge. Throughout this time, he encouraged the creation of literary, musical, and artistic pieces. Under his rule, the first Ottoman history manuscripts were completed by local historians.

In his final years, the sultan would be confronted by a challenge that would mark the beginning of the end of his reign. In the early 16th century, a new threat emerged in the east: the Safavid Persian Empire. The scenario was similar to the past. The Safavids had managed to quickly consolidate the Iranian territories under their control and eventually reached eastern Anatolia, conquering everyone on their way. Being Shia Muslims and followers of the Sufism movement, the Safavids confronted the Ottomans after they took control of Baghdad in 1504 and posed a threat to the principality of Dulkadir in eastern Turkey. Their agents, mainly Sufist Shia Imams (essentially Muslim priests), flocked into the Ottoman territories and started gaining a base of followers, gaining prominence among the Turks and instigating a series of revolts in 1511.

By this time, Sultan Bayezid had grown older and weaker, meaning that a change in leadership was necessary to deal with the Safavids. The sultan's policy toward the Iranians was one of appeasement, something that was regarded as cowardly by many in the empire. In early 1512, Prince Selim, the youngest of the sultan's three sons, convinced the Janissaries to support him in overthrowing his father. Selim forced Bayezid to abdicate, and the old sultan complied to avoid conflict and potential bloodshed. He declared Selim as the new Ottoman sultan and left Istanbul to spend the rest of his days in peace. Unfortunately, he died before he could arrive at his destination.

Selim the Grim

Sultan Selim was very unlike his father when it came to nearly everything, from personality to his decisions as a ruler. Unlike Bayezid, who, despite his victories in the wars against Christian vassals, was never too keen on warfare, Selim adopted a more aggressive, expansionist foreign policy, which was mainly driven by the Safavid domination in the east and the recent weakening of Ottoman influence in Anatolia. Thus, Selim's rule is characterized by the increased importance of the Janissary infantry, which was the core of the Ottoman army in the 16th century and had acted as one of the most instrumental tools when Selim seized power from Bayezid in early 1512. The decision to rely heavily on the Janissaries paid dividends for the sultan, who was confronted by external problems in the very first months of his reign.

In the east, the Safavids had united under a powerful ruler—Shah Ismail—and had taken over parts of eastern Anatolia, Georgia, and Syria. The conquered subjects of the Safavid Empire were forced to convert to Shia Islam and would soon make up the core of the empire's army. They came to be known as the Kizilbash ("redheads") for their infamous red headgear. They supported Shah Ismail in his goal of reuniting the historic Persian Empire, which spanned the territory from Central Asia to Jerusalem. Thus, Selim's and Ismail's interests directly clashed with each other, this time not only as the heads of two empires but also as representatives of the two main branches of Islam.

In Selim's early campaigns in eastern Anatolia, he encountered harsh resistance from the Shia Turkish population of the region. Just defeating the Kizilbash forces was not enough to guarantee their loyalty. Selim believed he needed to severely punish those who had changed their way of life and had converted, so he started destroying the social system that had been established after the Safavid conquest. The Shia Imams had done their jobs very well and had largely created an anti-Sunni sentiment in the traditionally Sunni peoples of eastern Anatolia. Nevertheless, Selim persevered. As he conquered the lost provinces and crushed the Safavid garrisons, he executed thousands of men and women whose attitudes, he thought, posed a problem to his rule.

Selim's ruthless campaign persisted until 1514, when he was finally confronted by a large Safavid army at the plain of Chaldiran. In a decisive battle, Selim managed to crush the Safavids, wounding and almost capturing Shah Ismail, who was forced to flee the battlefield. Only a few thousand Safavids survived from their initial number of forty thousand, giving the Ottomans direct access to further territories of the Safavid Empire, an opportunity that was quickly seized by Sultan Selim, who, for the first time in Ottoman history, managed to unify the eastern Anatolian provinces and even conquered parts of Iraq. Then, he pushed farther east into modern-day Azerbaijan, capturing the pivotal city of Tabriz, which significantly reduced the Safavid presence in the region.

A miniature depicting the Battle of Chaldiran.
https://commons.wikimedia.org/wiki/File:%22Shah_Ismail_at_the_Battle_of_Chaldiran%2
2,_from_Bijan%E2%80%99s_Tarikh-i_Jahangusha-yi_Khaqan_Sahibqiran.jpg

The sultan then followed up his victories with a brief halt of the offensive, having perhaps overtired his troops after months of constant fighting. Although the war with the Safavids was not officially over, Selim had managed to at least defeat the immediate threat of another invasion. So, he turned his attention to the south toward the Mamluks, who had long been one of the strongest Muslim empires in the world. The Mamluks had always been a thorn in the side of the Ottoman rulers, as they banked on every opportunity to weaken the Turks and increase their influence in the contested bordering region of Cilicia between Syria and the rest of Anatolia. The Mamluks, who held the Islamic holy sites of Mecca and Medina, were traditionally Sunni Muslims, but Selim nevertheless decided to wage war against them based on the fact they had supported the Shia Safavids in the conquests of the eastern Anatolian provinces.

Thus, Selim campaigned against the Egyptians, marching into Syria in early 1516. He was confronted by a large Mamluk army of no less than sixty thousand men north of Aleppo in August and engaged in one of the most decisive battles in history, as it determined the fate of the Middle East for centuries to come. In the Battle of Marj Dabiq, the Ottomans achieved a close victory against the Mamluks, thanks to their superior troops, and killed the Mamluk sultan, Qansuh al-Ghuri, routing the Egyptian army. Their victory led to the capture of several important cities, including Aleppo, Damascus, and Jerusalem.

By the end of 1516, the Ottoman conquests spanned the entire eastern coast of the Mediterranean, with Sultan Selim eventually reaching the Mamluk capital of Cairo in early 1517 after defeating the remainder of the Mamluk forces at the Battle of Ridaniya. The Ottomans had killed the new Mamluk sultan, Tuman bay II, in the battle and had come to the walls of Cairo with his head on a spike.

Thus, Cairo also fell to the Ottomans, followed by the rest of Egypt and the final holdings of the Mamluk Sultanate. After incorporating all these territories into his realm, Sultan Selim became the first Ottoman ruler to ever stretch the Ottoman Empire over three continents (Europe, Asia, and Africa). The Ottoman Empire was now the undisputed most powerful Islamic state in the world and finally held the holy sites of Mecca and Medina.

It was a pivotal moment in Ottoman history. Thanks to Selim's efforts, the empire now covered the most territory it had ever controlled. The victories against the Safavids and the conquest of the Mamluks ensured the emergence of the Ottoman Empire as perhaps the most powerful empire in the world. Selim had created an empire whose dominance would be very difficult to challenge due to its strong, modern, and disciplined army, which had years of field experience. His strict and ruthless nature also positively contributed to the establishment of the sultan's authority. Sultan Selim has come to be known as "the Grim" for his dreadful personality, but he was nevertheless a pivotal figure in the history of the Ottoman Empire.

Suleyman the Magnificent and the Ottoman Golden Age

Prince Suleyman (also spelled as Suleiman) ascended the throne after the death of Selim in 1520. The late sultan had made sure there would be no succession issues after his passing. As soon as he had become sultan himself, he slaughtered many of his family members, only leaving Suleyman alive as his true successor. Thus, the twenty-six-year-old Suleyman became the new sultan without any difficulties.

During his reign, the Ottoman Empire would reach the height of its power and truly become the most feared power in the world. For his incredible military, diplomatic, social, and economic achievements as sultan, Suleyman would be forever remembered as "the Magnificent." He was perhaps the greatest ruler in Ottoman history.

After taking over the realm, which had been greatly increased in size by his father, Suleyman sought to consolidate the gains in the Asian and African territories and also further expand in Europe. He asserted his dominance over Hungary, which would eventually give the Ottomans access to the heart of the continent. Reigniting the holy war was just the first step in Suleyman's pursual of world domination, a goal that had been set forth by his father.

The invasion of Hungary was justified thanks to several developments that had taken place in Europe in the 16th century, which had weakened the strength of the continent overall. Most importantly, the Protestant Reformation, which quickly spread throughout the German principalities of the Holy Roman Empire, saw the people become increasingly hostile toward the Catholic European states due to new religious differences and thoughts. The Reformation had rendered the calling of a new crusade against the Ottomans effectively impossible. And the Ottomans under Sultan Suleyman would try to capitalize on the Christians' religious strife by encouraging the promotion of Protestantism in Hungary, which lay open to an invasion, especially since it was ill-supported by their long-standing Christian allies.

In 1521, Suleyman campaigned against the remainder of the Christian nations in the Balkans, capturing Belgrade in August, which gave him control over the roads to southern Hungary. Then, in a shocking move, the sultan brokered an alliance with King Francis I of France. The French had hostile relations with the Habsburgs, who controlled not only the Holy Roman Empire but also Hungary. The alliance put more pressure on the Austrian house, which was, essentially, the common enemy of both the Ottomans and the French.

Following Suleyman's capture of Belgrade, he marched on the island of Rhodes, finally capturing the island from the Knights Hospitaller in January 1522. They had long troubled the Ottoman rulers due to their close ties with the Ottomans' enemies.

Suleyman (or Suleiman) the Magnificent.
https://commons.wikimedia.org/wiki/File:EmperorSuleiman.jpg

Three years later, the rivalry between Francis I and Charles V of the Holy Roman Empire erupted into an all-out war, and the sultan's assistance was needed after the French king was captured in the summer of 1525. Suleyman thrust into the Habsburg-controlled Hungarian territories. With the defeat of King Louis II of Hungary at the decisive Battle of Mohács in August 1526, Sultan Suleyman broke the heart of the Hungarian army and sealed the fate of the Hungarian state. With their king slain on the battlefield, the Hungarian cities fell one by one. Most notably, Suleyman's forces sacked the city of Buda in September and took over much of the southern Hungarian territories. The Ottoman sultan even desired to capture Vienna, which he did besiege upon the renewal of his campaign in 1529. However, he was forced to abandon the siege in October due to extreme weather conditions that created supply problems for his army. Nevertheless, by 1530, Sultan Suleyman had expanded his realm into eastern Europe, exploiting the weakness of the Christian world.

The next thing on his agenda was to establish naval supremacy in the Mediterranean, where Venice and Genoa, despite the losses of their colonies in the late 15th century, still remained dominant. Famously, Suleyman appointed Hayreddin Barbarossa, a former corsair, as his admiral and charged him with the fleet that would take over the seas from the Italians. Under Hayreddin Barbarossa's leadership, the Ottoman forces conquered Tunis in 1534, taking control over most of the North African coast. Then, in 1538, Hayreddin Barbarossa decisively defeated a Christian coalition of Venice and Naples that had been called by Pope Paul III in the naval Battle of Preveza, despite the numerical advantage the Christians held. With the victory at Preveza, as well as the capture of the Venetian-held island of Corfu a year earlier by the joint Ottoman-Franco forces, Suleyman had managed to truly assert his dominance in the Mediterranean, forcing Venice to sue for peace in 1540.

After expanding his realm in Europe by capturing parts of Hungary and Croatia, including the city of Budapest, and after undermining the supremacy of the Venetians in the Mediterranean, Sultan Suleyman finally had time to address another one of his problems: the Safavids. The Safavids had largely been confined to

Iran after Selim's victories against them, but Shia Muslims were still present in Iraq, Azerbaijan, and the South Caucasus, which directly bordered Ottoman territories. Since the official peace treaty between the two sides had never been signed, small-scale skirmishes between the Ottomans and the Safavids regularly broke out, something the sultan sought to end once and for all. In addition, some European nations, like Portugal, Spain, and Venice, which were bothered by the growing power of the Ottomans in the Mediterranean and the Middle East, had tried to counterbalance the situation by getting on good terms with the Safavids in the hopes of undermining Ottoman strength in the contested regions.

To truly choke out the Safavids from Mesopotamia and the Near East, the sultan believed the best course of action was an offensive on Baghdad and Basra, which would allow the Ottomans to reach the Persian Gulf and make it easier for them to challenge the Europeans and Safavids in the Indian Ocean while also opening up new trade opportunities for the empire.

In 1533, parallel to his war against the Venetians, Sultan Suleyman started his campaign in Iran. But the Safavids, having learned from their crushing defeat at the hands of Sultan Selim at Chaldiran, decided not to confront the mighty Ottoman army in an open field. Instead, the Safavids, under the leadership of Shah Tahmasp, retreated from their westernmost territories and adopted a scorched-earth policy, burning everything that could have been utilized by the Ottomans to the ground. The Safavids hoped that Suleyman would change his mind and halt his offensive.

However, despite their best efforts, Sultan Suleyman refused to go back, and in 1534, he marched into Azerbaijan. The Ottomans reestablished their rule over the city of Tabriz before pivoting south and capturing Mesopotamia, including the city of Baghdad, which fell into Ottoman hands without much fighting in November.

With Baghdad and Tabriz under his belt, Sultan Suleyman consolidated his easternmost holdings. The Ottoman Empire now held control over the most important cities west of the Caspian Sea and dominated the historical region of the Levant. The Ottoman Empire would hold onto these territories until World War I. Still, despite taking over these lands, Sultan Suleyman couldn't destroy the core of Safavid Iran, and he did not want to risk overextending himself in the east when he had other campaigns underway in the Mediterranean.

So, the sultan decided to wait. While skirmishes between the Ottomans and the Safavids persisted, a large Ottoman force would again invade the Safavid lands in 1548. This time, Suleyman hoped to exploit the Safavids, who had been engulfed in dynastical wars and faced domestic problems. Alqas Mirza, brother of Shah Tahmasp, had fled to the Ottomans to ask for political asylum, urging the sultan to go to war for his claim on the Safavid throne.

However, this expedition was doomed from the start. Suleyman did not lead his men himself, giving over the control of his army to Alqas Mirza, who was not a particularly good commander. The Safavids repelled the Ottoman campaigns until 1555, when the two sides signed the Treaty of Amasya, finally putting an end to more than half a decade of war. According to the terms of the treaty, the two sides equally divided Armenia and Georgia. The Safavids also regained control of Tabriz, their former capital, while the Ottomans retained possession of their Iraqi conquests, including the cities of Mosul, Baghdad, and Basra.

It is not surprising that Sultan Suleyman was referred to by his contemporaries as "the Magnificent" for his achievements. By the time of his death in 1566, he was by far the most powerful man in Europe, with the Ottoman Empire spanning the Balkans, Anatolia, the Levant, Hijaz, and the North African coast. The empire had vassals in Wallachia, Moldavia, Georgia, and Transylvania. Suleyman managed to build upon the conquests of his father, further consolidating his power in the newly acquired territories and pushing farther into Europe than any of his predecessors. He cleverly utilized the sociopolitical turmoil of the Christian nations that had historically opposed the Ottomans. By constructing a mighty army and, for the first time, a mighty navy, Sultan Suleyman was certainly one of the most iconic and magnificent Ottoman rulers.

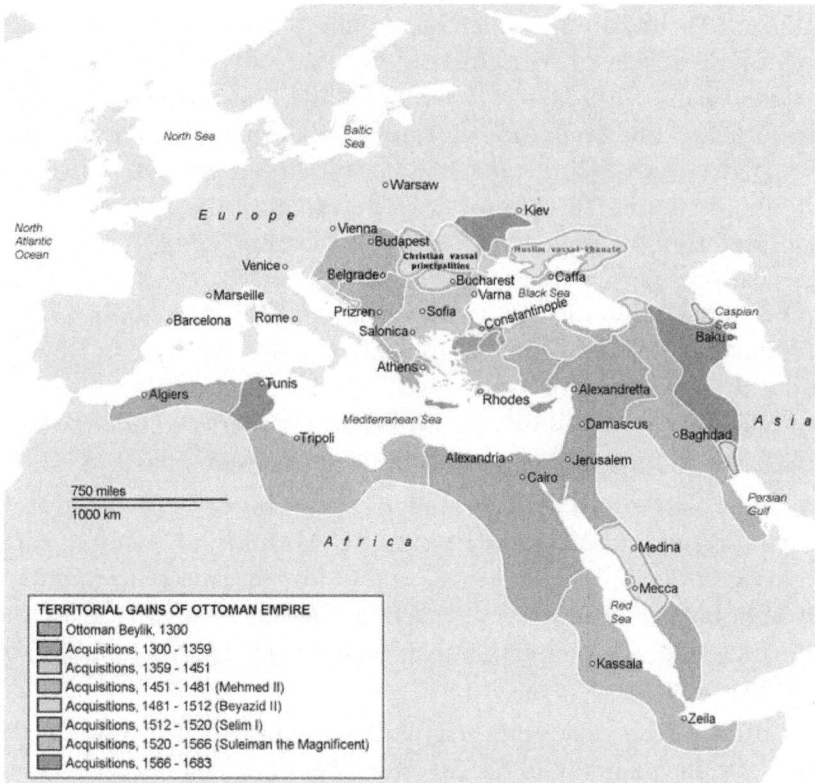

Expansion of the Ottoman Empire.
https://commons.wikimedia.org/wiki/File:OttomanEmpireIn1683.png

However, Suleyman is not only well remembered for his territorial conquests. While he was known in the west as "the Magnificent," in his realm, he was often referred to as "the Lawgiver" due to the social and legal reforms he implemented throughout his reign. Although he did not significantly alter the sacred Sharia, the Islamic law, which had long been one of the foundations of the empire, Sultan Suleyman did introduce a new, more coherent legal code, building on traditions while adopting changes fit for his empire. His *qanuns* ("dynastic laws") touched upon many aspects of everyday life and improved administrative systems, such as taxation and criminal law. These changes effectively helped the empire's economic and social growth, taking it to new heights.

In addition to the legal reforms, Sultan Suleyman contributed greatly to the development of arts and culture in the Ottoman

Empire. As an admirer of literature and a poet, Suleyman's reign saw a golden age of Muslim culture. The sultan cordially invited various artists to his palace to work on different projects, encouraging the youth to start their apprenticeships with more experienced artists and pursue their careers to further enrich the Ottoman culture. The Crown started to finance the construction of several mosques, aqueducts, and architectural complexes, and it also paid artisans, painters, and writers directly from the treasury. Some of the most amazing Ottoman architecture was a direct result of Suleyman, including the famous Süleymaniye Mosque in Istanbul and the mosque of Edirne, both of which have become great symbols of the Ottoman Empire's prosperity under Sultan Suleyman. They continue to fascinate visitors even today.

All in all, there have been few rulers in history who deserve as much praise as Sultan Suleyman the Magnificent, who is most deserving of his title. He elevated the Ottoman Empire to the status of a global superpower. A smart diplomat, great strategist, avid reformer, and a noble man, Sultan Suleyman's legacy is full of glory and prosperity.

Unfortunately, after the heights the empire reached during the reign of Suleyman, the Ottomans were doomed to suffer a period of instability and regress, something that would slowly contribute to its decline.

Chapter 5: Decline of the Empire

In the span of 150 years, the Ottoman Empire went from being just a regional power to a global hegemon. By the time of Sultan Suleyman's death in 1566, the empire spanned three continents, possessed a huge army and a competent navy, controlled some of the world's most valuable trade routes, and was feared by its rivals. However, historians generally agree that the decline of the Ottoman Empire slowly began after Suleyman, during the reign of his son, Selim II, who could not manage to even partially live up to his father's name.

This chapter will look at the tumultuous period after Sultan Suleyman's reign and examine some of the causes behind the empire's slow decline.

Old Wars, New Enemies

The late sultan had named his second eldest son, Selim, as his successor, who had also been his favorite of the two. Perhaps this was Suleyman's worst decision, as Selim was unlike his father in almost every aspect. He lacked Suleyman's charm, diligence, and strength of character. Instead, the new sultan was often called Sarhoş, meaning "Drunkard," because of his love for wine and women. Since Selim spent most of his time drinking and partying, influence in the court was assumed by Sokollu Mehmed Pasha, who had been Sultan Suleyman's grand vizier and helped raise Selim when he was young. Additionally, Selim's influence was also undermined by his favorite wife, Nurbanu, who would often make decisions on behalf of her husband. Due to this carelessness toward ruling, Selim is not exactly remembered as a good sultan.

However, despite this, the first years of Selim II's reign saw the continuation of the Ottoman expansionist policies, which had now become a tradition for the realm. The Ottoman armies campaigned in Yemen and reestablished the sultan's rule in the southern Arabian Peninsula in 1568, giving the empire more control over the Red Sea. Next, the Ottomans tried to take the city of Astrakhan, north of the Caspian Sea, to extend the empire's reach beyond the Caucasus Mountains. However, despite their best efforts, it was clear from the beginning of the campaign that the Ottomans were overreaching, as they heavily relied on their Crimean vassals to help them with the offensives in regions where Iranian and Russian influence was the most prominent. Thus, the Ottomans eventually abandoned their hopes and instead turned their attention to the island of Cyprus, which had served as a long-standing safe haven for the pirates of the Mediterranean.

By 1571, Cyprus had fallen to Selim, but instead of it leading to the consolidation of Ottoman power in the region, the fall of Cyprus incited the creation of another Holy League against the Ottomans. The fall of Cyprus reignited the wars between the Ottoman Empire and the Habsburgs, as well as between the Ottomans and the Venetians, the latter of whom provided the Christians with a large enough fleet to launch a naval attack on the Turks. In October 1571, the Christians trapped the Ottoman ships at Lepanto on the Greek coast, destroying most of Selim's fleet and achieving a decisive victory. The Battle of Lepanto was one of the biggest defeats in Ottoman history and resulted in the loss of morale in the Ottoman forces. Still, the empire's resources were immense, even when compared to the combined strength of the Holy League. Furious with the defeat, Selim ordered the complete reconstruction of his navy and, in about a year, retaliated brilliantly against the Christians. In 1573, the Ottoman naval attacks on Venice caused the latter to sue for peace separately from the Holy League, leaving the rest without their most powerful ally.

Selim II passed away in 1574, with the throne going to his son, Murad III, who ruled for twenty-one years. Murad III was much like his father, as he had tens of different concubines and, according to some narratives, more than one hundred sons and daughters throughout his time as sultan. This naturally produced rivalries in the sultan's harem—the part of the household that was reserved for the women of the family—as different wives, concubines, and their children struggled to become Murad's favorite. These rivalries, which were essentially produced from jealousies toward each other, eventually resulted in the creation of factions in the sultan's court. The factions tried to influence Murad when it came to important political matters.

During the first part of Sultan Murad's reign, he heavily relied on his grand vizier, Sokollu Mehmed, who had also served as grand vizier to Selim II. Thanks to the efforts of Sokollu Mehmed, a smart political figure, the Ottoman Empire was able to achieve several triumphs in the early years of Murad III's time as sultan. The grand vizier made sure to extend the peace agreements with the empire's European rivals—the Habsburgs, Venice, and Poland—and launched a military campaign in North Africa to invade and successfully occupy Morocco in 1576. This conquest not only gave Murad control over all of the North African coast but also gave the Ottomans more naval power in the Mediterranean. It allowed the Ottomans to undermine the Portuguese, Spanish, and French in the western Mediterranean, eventually leading to the empire striking a trade agreement with England in 1580 to let English merchants conduct business in Ottoman lands with relative freedom. Sokollu Mehmed saw England as a rival to all these western European nations, so he believed that good relations with the English would allow the Ottomans to become the dominant commercial actor in the region once again.

The grand vizier would meet his end during the ambitious military campaign to invade Safavid Iran, which began in 1578. Although Sokollu Mehmed was personally against an expedition so far east, the factions in the sultan's court had convinced Murad to capitalize on the weakness of the Safavid state and take over the territories once conquered by Sultan Suleyman. The sultan was especially swayed by the *ulama*, the Muslim scholars who specialized in Islamic law and regarded the Shia Safavids as a traditional enemy of the empire. Thus, the Ottoman forces launched a massive campaign into the territories controlled by Iran, gaining control of Georgia and Armenia, which had been divided by the Treaty of Amasya in 1555. The Ottomans also gained the Caucasian provinces of Dagestan, Shirvan, and Karabakh.

However, a year later, in October 1579, the grand vizier was assassinated by his rivals in court, who were perhaps jealous of his successes in the war against the Safavids. Still, the Ottoman-Safavid conflict lasted for another ten years until Murad III finally forced Shah Abbas, the ruler of Iran, to sue for peace in 1590, thanks to support from the Sunni Uzbeks, who attacked the Safavids from the northeast. The Ottomans took over the westernmost Safavid territories, and the riches seized from the campaign refilled the royal treasury.

Internal Problems

These relative successes when it came to military campaigns masked the array of internal problems the Ottoman Empire faced. We have already noted the problems in the administration and governance of the empire, as different factions had emerged in court, trying to wrestle power from each other to gain the favor of the sultan and make the most important political decisions. However, the roots of these problems went far deeper than harem rivalries and the sultan's preferences. Instead, the problem partially lay in the corrupt bureaucratic system of the empire, which was now, more than ever, comprised of the devshirme instead of Turkish nobility. Corruption spread like wildfire, and different actors tried to exert their influence on the sultans from behind the scenes. It did not matter who exactly controlled the government since the Ottoman Empire was inherently an autocratic empire, which meant the ruler held unlimited power. A weak sultan meant a weak realm.

By the end of the 16ᵗʰ century, the empire suffered economic difficulties. Yes, through their conquests, the Ottomans had increased their presence in the Mediterranean and in the western Indian Ocean, but with the start of the Age of Exploration, international trade routes soon shifted from the territories controlled by the Ottomans. Many Catholic factions did not trust the Muslim Ottomans when trying to conduct trade with Asia, choosing instead to find new routes to the Asian markets that would circumvent Ottoman holdings. The Ottoman Empire's total control of the Middle East was one of the reasons behind the Spanish, Portuguese, English, Dutch, and French efforts to invest in world exploration, as they hoped to avoid confrontations with the Ottomans when conducting trade. Soon enough, with the discoveries and exploitation of new markets in the Americas and Asia, the Ottoman economy started to decline.

These developments precipitated domestic economic problems that affected most of the Ottoman population, especially the people who were dependent on wages. Inflation soared since the Ottoman market was unable to keep up with the ever-growing European economies, and traditional industries started to decrease in their effectiveness. When paired with the high levels of corruption and exploitation of property and labor by powerful Ottoman officials, the economic turmoil of the empire resulted in a multitude of social problems, reducing many to poverty. This, unfortunately, coincided with high levels of population growth, meaning that more and more people were being born but faced very tough living conditions, especially in the countryside. Agricultural production stagnated, as underpayment of peasants caused food shortages around the realm, causing many to flee to the cities to try and survive, which, in turn, caused urban unrest and increased rates of crime.

Ignoring these problems only increased their severity, as the poor, starving peasants-turned-criminals organized themselves into bands. They terrorized the Ottoman countryside and further contributed to the country's instability. Referred to as the Celali, they became very dangerous, posing a threat to supply chains and undermining the garrisons due to their superior numbers. The Celali rebellions, which erupted throughout the country multiple times from the late 16th century to the mid-17th century, weakened the central government and caused almost the complete disorganization of the Ottoman military.

In the latter half of Murad III's reign, he could not pay the upkeep for his elite and core Janissary corps, which had made up the bulk of the Ottoman army for centuries. Instead, he had to rely heavily on inexperienced, cheaper levies, which he could muster up in times of need, and the Crimean forces provided by his vassals. Due to all of these problems, Murad's victory in Iran was pivotal in maintaining control of the empire, which was in a very difficult state overall.

Mehmed III and Ahmed I

Thus, the gradual, painful decline of the Ottoman Empire from the inside out persisted after the reign of Sultan Suleyman. Although Murad III's victory against the Safavids was a temporary sigh of relief for the Ottomans, it by no means meant that all their problems would go away. What the empire needed was an all-out reform, a series of changes that would touch almost every aspect of Ottoman life and fundamentally transform the domestic situation. In fact, the mid-17th century would see the first Ottoman sultans with the zeal to address some of the empire's problems, but before that happened, Mehmed III and Ahmed I would ascend the throne. Both sultans' reigns would see important developments that further weakened the Ottomans.

Mehmed III, the son of Murad III, became the new sultan in 1595 after the passing of his father. Eccentric, strict, and borderline crazy, Mehmed III started his reign by slaughtering half of his family since he did not trust them, although it is possible he was under the influence of well-established factions in the harem. Much like his father, the grand vizier would see his powers grow greatly during Mehmed's reign.

In early 1596, Mehmed was engaged in a war against two of his European vassals, Moldavia and Wallachia, as they had increasingly been influenced by the Habsburgs to break free from Ottoman rule. Unable to defeat the vassals on the first try, the Ottomans asked for the Crimean Tatars' help in their war, something that, in turn, caused the Kingdom of Poland to intervene. The Polish believed that the Muslims posed a threat to the security in the region. Despite the Celali rebellions and the Polish defending the Christians from the Tatar invasions in the north, Mehmed III's armies achieved several victories against the Habsburgs throughout 1596, most importantly at the Battle of Keresztes against Maximillian III of the Holy Roman Empire in October.

However, Mehmed was unable to establish firm control over the Wallachian and Moldavian territories, as the unrest back home made it impossible to wage external wars. The Ottoman army was disorganized and weak, something that had become clear during the wars and could potentially be exploited in the future. Temporary order was established, but it was clear that, sooner or later, the Ottoman power would dwindle in the region.

In 1603, Mehmed III was succeeded by his son, Ahmed I, after he suffered a sudden stroke. The thirteen-year-old Ahmed was confronted with immense pressure from everywhere. The Habsburgs were keen on wrestling the control of Transylvania from the Ottomans, Shah Abbas of the Safavids had reconsolidated his power and was starting to wage a vengeful war against the sultan, and, last but not least, domestic chaos and instability had reached its peak.

The sultan first started by dealing with the Habsburg threat, which, as his court believed, was the easiest among the three to deal with. In 1604, the Ottoman forces saw some success against the Habsburgs, capturing the city of Pest. Then, with Transylvanian Prince Stephen Bocskai's help, the Ottomans drove the Habsburg forces from the contested regions, signing the Treaty of Zsitvatorok in November 1606 to end the conflict between the two sides. Transylvania became an Ottoman vassal once again, and Ahmed reestablished his control of the territories north of the Danube River.

Then, it was time to turn his attention to the east, where Shah Abbas had retaliated after his defeat by the Ottomans in 1590. He had fully retrained and reorganized his Kizilbash army, largely basing it on the Ottoman Janissaries. With this new structure in place, he defeated the Uzbek Sunnis in the first years of the 1600s. Shah Abbas and his experienced and professional force marched west, taking back the territories conquered by Murad III and destroying the Ottoman garrisons in Azerbaijan, the Caucasus, western Iran, and eastern Anatolia. By 1604, the Safavids had besieged and taken Yerevan and Kars while the sultan had been occupied by the Habsburgs. The Safavids established a base of operations in Armenia and posed a real threat to the Ottoman heartland.

It was clear the Safavids had abandoned their defensive approach to the Ottomans, who had dominated them for almost a century.

With Shah Abbas at the Ottoman Empire's doorstep, Sultan Ahmed I needed to act. Marvelously, despite the social unrest present in the country at that time, the sultan was able to mobilize one of the largest Ottoman forces of all time, counting no less than eighty thousand men, and marched on the Safavids in 1605. However, in September, as the two armies confronted each other near Lake Urmia in northwestern Iraq, it became clear the Ottomans were outclassed. The reorganized forces of Shah Abbas crushed the Turks on the battlefield, slaying more than twenty thousand and capturing many more.

As the Ottomans retreated, Shah Abbas used the opportunity to seize even more territories, capturing the cities of Baghdad and Najaf and establishing Safavid rule over most of Iraq and Kurdistan. After the defeat of the Ottomans, many Turkish princes who had previously been under the sultan's rule defected to the shah, converting to Shia Islam and pledging allegiance to the Safavid ruler, who had defeated the Ottomans and become their equal.

Devastated by the loss, Ahmed I ordered his grand vizier, Murad Pasha, to muster another army and tasked him with retaliating against the Safavids. Before the grand vizier took on the Iranians, he gathered the new men and brutally suppressed the ongoing Celali rebellions in Anatolia and the Balkans. By late 1608, most of the rebels had either been captured or massacred by the Ottoman armies under Murad Pasha, who then finally marched against the Safavids in the east.

Instead of fighting with the Ottomans, Shah Abbas retreated from eastern Anatolia and Armenia, burning villages, destroying supplies, and forcing the local populations to flee eastward to render the Ottoman efforts useless. This made it impossible for the Ottomans to wage a long-term war against the Safavids, as they were unable to stretch their supply lines that far east.

Despite Murad Pasha's attempts, he was unable to catch up with Shah Abbas. Murad Pasha died in 1611, forcing Ahmed I to halt the offensive and accept a peace treaty with the Safavids a year later. According to the terms of the peace, Ahmed recognized all the Safavid conquests and declared Shah Abbas as the ruler of the Caucasus and Azerbaijan.

Early Reforms

Ahmed I passed away in 1617, a year after he had renewed the war with Iran over Armenia. By the time Osman II ascended the throne in 1618, Ottoman power had dwindled significantly, and its rivals had certainly noticed it. Constant wars on all fronts rendered the Ottomans weaker than ever, and fundamental domestic changes were necessary to make sure the empire avoided total collapse. For the rest of the 17th century, as multiple Ottoman sultans came and went, there were signs of life when it came to internal reforms. Ultimately, however, by the end of the 17th century, although some immediate problematic matters were dealt with, the Ottoman Empire had still not recovered the position it had held a hundred years earlier.

Murad IV, who became the sultan at the age of eleven in 1623, was perhaps the most competent Ottoman ruler of the 17th century. During his reign, much of the corruption within the administrative system would be rooted out. Since the early days of his reign, Murad was confronted with the renewed conflict with the Safavids, who had once again thrust into Iraq and massacred the Sunni population of Baghdad in 1624. Despite the Ottomans' efforts to retake the city and defeat the Iranians, the two eastern campaigns in the following years failed, creating even more problems within the empire and causing unrest in the higher ranks of Ottoman society. Members of the Janissary and the *sipahi* (cavalry) corps of the army were discontent with the continued defeats the army suffered. And after their commander, Grand Vizier Hüsrev Pasha, was dismissed by Murad in 1631, they tried to instigate an all-out rebellion against the sultan. Aided by many high-ranking officials, the military entered Istanbul and massacred many of the sultan's closest allies in court, including the new grand vizier, giving way to mass protests all around the city. Murad had a rather chaotic situation to deal with.

Surprisingly, thanks to the strength of his character, the new sultan quickly consolidated his power, demanding that the rebellious troops swear loyalty to him. He ordered them to execute those bureaucrats whom he believed were treacherous toward the Crown. By the autumn of 1633, the bandits and criminals that had ravaged the streets of Istanbul had been dealt with, as they had been thrown into the dungeons along with many of the corrupt officeholders.

When a large portion of the capital burned down due to a large fire, Murad claimed that it was a bad omen from God, a sign of his wrath. The sultan used the fire to restore some moral order in the empire. He banned the usage of tobacco and coffee and closed down many shops that had been used as gathering places by protesters. He also organized a complex spy network that was tasked with identifying enemies of the Crown, resulting in the arrests and executions of thousands of officials, servicemen, and members of the *ulama.*

Crucially, before his death in 1640, Murad managed to recapture much of Iraq and sign a new peace deal with the Safavids, dividing the border territories between the two empires largely along the lines of the Treaty of Amasya of 1555. The death of Shah Abbas weakened the Iranian state, allowing Murad to launch a four-year-long campaign that eventually resulted in an Ottoman victory.

With much of the corruption dealt with and the Safavids in the east neutralized, at least for the time being, it seemed as if the Ottoman Empire was starting to come back to its full strength. However, for the next few decades, due to weak sultans under the influence of their harems and pashas (essentially a prime minister or grand vizier), it became clear the Ottomans had significantly fallen behind their European counterparts in regard to development and modernization.

One of the most interesting developments in the empire during these troubled times was the so-called Köprülü Era, which started in 1656 and lasted for nearly three decades. During this period, the office of the grand vizier was occupied by members of the Köprülü family, something that was largely due to the efforts of Köprülü Mehmed Pasha, who had been appointed as grand vizier during Mehmed IV's reign in 1656. Before Köprülü's time in office, Tarhoncu Ahmed Pasha had led the realm in economic reforms, completely reorganizing the treasury, which had been depleted by constant wars. He made sure to imprison all of the corrupt members of the imperial elite, confiscating their lands and wealth and refilling the royal treasury. Large estates held by a few powerful men in court were redistributed to ensure economic growth. New taxes were implemented, and the budget for the fiscal year was determined for the first time in Ottoman history. In short, Tarhoncu Ahmed Pasha greatly contributed to the reorganization of the Ottoman economy and centralization of power before his dismissal in 1653 after false rumors that he had tried to overthrow the sultan.

After three years of political instability, Köprülü Mehmed Pasha became the new grand vizier and soon emerged as the most powerful man in the realm, with the next few grand viziers coming from his family. Köprülü Mehmed Pasha personally replaced the high-ranking officials of the empire with those he trusted. After gaining solid control over the government, the grand vizier enjoyed freedom in making the political decisions of the empire and even drove out the Venetians from the Dardanelles in July 1657. Then, he led the realm against the rebelling Transylvanian princes, who were finally dealt with in 1662, restoring Ottoman suzerainty in the region.

Under his successors, the Ottoman Empire managed to expand farther into Europe, capturing Polish territories in Ukraine in 1676, defeating the Habsburg-led Christian coalition in 1664, and capturing Crete from Venice in 1669. Throughout all of this, the grand viziers held tight control over the offices of the empire, not allowing corruption to spread more within the realm.

Chapter 6: The First Losses of the Empire

During the 17th century, the Ottoman Empire experienced domestic and external challenges, which slowly became increasingly difficult to deal with. As weaker sultans ascended the throne, court intrigues and behind-the-scenes actors would take control of the decision-making within the empire, something that produced mixed results. This chapter will talk about the significant defeats the empire suffered throughout the 18th century, a period when the rest of Europe championed absolutism. These defeats would eventually prove costly to the Ottomans, leading to the empire's decline and its late push for modernization.

The Disaster at Vienna

By the 1680s, the grand viziers from the Köprülü family had become the masters in the Ottoman Empire, destroying any opposition in court and essentially becoming the true despots of the realm. The conquest of western Ukraine in the late 1670s under Kara Mustafa Pasha alarmed the Russians, who saw the Muslim Ottomans on their doorstep as a direct threat. The two sides confronted each other, and in February 1681, the Ottomans agreed to sign a peace deal, renouncing their claims in Ukraine and retreating.

However, this decision did not necessarily mean the Russians had overpowered the Turks. Instead, the grand vizier recognized the instability in Habsburg Hungary, believing the rebellions against the ruling family were his chance to march upon Vienna and take the rich city. Motivated by their French allies in the west, who were just as adamant about seeing the Habsburgs collapse, the Ottomans invaded the Austrian territories in 1683, laying siege to Vienna in June. Vienna had long been a bastion of Christian defense against the Ottomans ever since the conquests of Selim and Suleyman in the 16th century, two sultans who had come dangerously close to capturing the city. Having more than 100,000 men at his disposal, the grand vizier hoped the city would fall, believing the Habsburg armies had been weakened by constant fighting against the rebels.

Battle of Vienna.
https://commons.wikimedia.org/wiki/File:Vienna_Battle_1683.jpg

However, the Habsburgs had organized an anti-Ottoman coalition, recognizing the threat that would be imposed on the Christian world if Vienna fell to the Ottomans. With support from King John III Sobieski of Poland-Lithuania, the Papal States, and several Holy Roman princes, Holy Roman Emperor Leopold I was able to arrive at the city with a relief force of more than eighty thousand troops. In September, after three months of the siege, just as the Ottomans had bombarded the city walls enough to push through and take it, the Christians were able to launch a surprise attack, routing the Ottoman forces and achieving victory. The grand vizier had come dangerously close to capturing Vienna, much closer than his ancestors in 1529. Humiliated, the Ottoman forces retreated, leaving behind their cannons, equipment, and supplies. Upon his return to Istanbul, the grand vizier was executed by Sultan Mehmed IV.

The failure to capture Vienna was the beginning of the end for the Ottomans' power in Europe. The Ottoman army had completely disintegrated, allowing the Habsburgs to lead a campaign deep inside Ottoman-controlled territories. Now joined by the Italian states, the Habsburgs' Christian coalition launched a decisive offensive, liberating the towns under the Ottoman yoke and taking Budapest in 1686.

Military Troubles

While the Ottomans were slowly losing their grip in most of Hungary, they had more success defending their positions in the northeast against the Polish in Moldavia, where they repelled John Sobieski in 1687. The Christians retaliated, as Venice, with Habsburg support, managed to take a portion of the Dalmatian coast from the Ottomans and capture the fortress of Morea. By September of 1687, the Venetians had invaded Greece and taken Athens, something that greatly alarmed the Ottoman government in Istanbul. The Muslim population of the captured regions fled to the Ottoman mainland, flocking to the big cities in southern Thrace and causing even more social unrest, in addition to the economic turmoil that was caused by the decrease in agricultural production.

As the 17th century came to an end, the Ottoman Empire's problems only increased in numbers and severity. After the loss of Budapest and the defeat at Vienna, Mehmed IV's reputation was destroyed beyond repair. Thus, the grand vizier, along with the powerful actors in court, instigated a quick revolution, deposing the sultan and placing Sultan Ibrahim's son, Suleyman, as the new ruler in 1687. However, this move only made it clearer to the empire's enemies that the Ottomans were weak at their core, leading to a series of Christian campaigns in the Balkans. Although the new sultan tried to sue for peace with the Habsburgs, by the fall of 1689, Emperor Leopold had thrust deep into the Ottoman-controlled territories, having captured the cities of Niš, Vidin, and Skopje. Although the Ottomans, under Grand Vizier Fazil Mustafa Pasha, retaliated a year later, recapturing Niš and Belgrade from the Habsburgs, after the death of Suleyman II and the recontinuation of hostilities under Sultan Ahmed II, the Habsburgs decisively defeated the remainder of the Ottoman armies at Slankamen in August 1691.

The victorious Christian coalition, consisting of the Habsburgs, Venice, Poland, and Russia, continued to heavily pressure the Ottoman holdings in eastern Europe, launching offensives on all sides. Ahmed II passed away in 1695, leaving the realm to his son, Mustafa II, who was adamant about driving out the Habsburgs from the lost territories. However, his attacks against the Austrians ended disastrously, as the Ottomans suffered a crushing defeat at the Battle of Zenta in September 1697 against the Habsburg forces under Eugene of Savoy. Russia's Peter the Great had also taken Ottoman lands on the northern Black Sea coast in 1696, and defeat after defeat forced Ahmed II to sue for a humiliating peace against the Christians.

The Treaty of Karlowitz (Carlowitz), which was signed in January 1699 between the Ottomans on one side and Venice, Russia, Poland, and the Habsburg monarchy on the other, marked the end of Ottoman dominance in southeastern Europe. The Ottomans lost Dalmatia and the Morea to Venice, western Ukraine and Podolia to Poland, Azov to Russia, and most of Hungary and Transylvania to the Habsburgs. The sultan also agreed to guarantee the freedoms of the Christian subjects in his realm. The treaty was a clear sign that the balance of power had shifted against the Ottoman Empire, which had been the dominant force in the region for a long time.

Despite the "peace" with the empire's Christian rivals, the Ottomans went to war with each of them several times throughout the 18th century. While it is impossible to cover all the developments of these conflicts in great detail, it is possible to find an underlying unifying characteristic. One word perhaps best describes the Ottoman military endeavors in the 1700s: disappointment. In the Austro-Turkish War of 1716-1718 and the Austro-Russian-Turkish War of 1735-1739, the once-mighty Ottoman army was unable to put up enough resistance to overcome the Christians. The first half of the century saw mixed results when it came to controlling the empire's contested peripheral territories. After suffering a defeat against Austria, the Treaty of Passarowitz in 1718 stripped the Ottoman Empire of much of its Balkan holdings, including Serbia and western Romania. The Treaty of Belgrade, signed in 1739, saw the restoration of Ottoman control to some of these lands (this time around, the Ottomans had managed to defeat the Habsburgs). The treaty also ceded the control of a portion of the northern Black Sea coast to Russia. All in all, it was a chaotic first half of the century when it came to foreign wars. The contested regions were greatly destabilized due to all the fighting, causing mass migration and sharp falls in production.

In addition to the wars in Europe, the 1730s also saw the Ottomans clash with the Safavids, who had regained their strength. The Shia empire invaded the Middle Eastern and Caucasian territories under the control of the Ottoman Empire, prompting Sultan Mahmud I to send large forces to deal with the Iranians. This move divided the Ottoman army in half, with the other part fighting in Europe. Although the Ottomans saw some success after fighting broke out in Iraq, under Nader, the Safavid shah's right hand and chief minister, the Shias retaliated and managed to capture Baghdad before laying siege and seizing Yerevan, Tbilisi, and Ganja. In 1736, the Ottomans sued for peace, which only lasted for about nine years, as, in 1745, the Safavids renewed their offensive for another year, eventually resulting in another peace agreement in 1746, which stopped the fighting between the two Muslim empires.

Surprisingly, during the 1740s to the late 1760s, the Ottoman Empire finally found itself at peace, despite the fact that its neighbors were engulfed in the Seven Years' War and the War for the Austrian Succession, two defining conflicts of the 18th century. However, the Ottoman sultans of the time were unable to use this opportunity to address the fundamental problems within the empire. The army, which for centuries had enjoyed both numerical and technological superiority when compared to its counterparts, needed reorganization. The more disciplined European forces often overpowered the old-fashioned Ottoman military during their encounters on the battlefield. Furthermore, the central government had lost its firm grip over its subjects and needed strengthening. However, inaction precipitated one of the most difficult periods the

Ottomans would have to face. From the latter half of the 18th century to World War I, as the European nations rose to the height of their power in the age of imperialism and nationalism, the Ottoman Empire could not adapt to the ever-changing world order, leading to the final stages of its decline.

The Modernization Problem

From 1768 to 1774, the Ottoman Empire saw itself go to war with Russia once again. Over the past one hundred years, the Russians had emerged as one of the most powerful empires of Europe and, under Catherine the Great, had reached the height of their power. Seeing itself as the defender of the Orthodox Christian faith and a big brother to all the Slavic nations of the Balkans, Russia had shown increasing interest when it came to the politics of the region and had been involved in wars over those lands for the past century. In 1768, after the assaults on the Ottoman-controlled territories in Moldavia, the Ottomans declared war on Russia. In six years, the Ottomans suffered a rather decisive defeat at the hands of Catherine the Great.

When the peace agreement between the two sides was signed in July 1774, the Crimean Khanate, which had historically been a vassal and an ally of the Ottoman Empire, was liberated. Technically, neither Russia nor the Ottomans had the right to influence Crimea according to the treaty, but the Crimean Tatars were eventually annexed by Russia by the end of the 18th century. In addition, the Russians received important Black Sea port cities, namely Azov and Kerch, as well as parts of Ottoman Moldavia and war reparations. Crucially, the Ottomans were forced to declare Russia as the protector of all Orthodox Ottoman subjects, a special status Russia assumed proudly and exercised for many years.

By the end of the century, the Ottomans went to war with Russia and the Habsburgs several times, although the conflicts always ended in disappointment for the Muslims. The Turks lost control of the Caucasus and the northern Black Sea coast to the Russians and gave up parts of Wallachia, Bosnia, and Serbia to the Habsburg monarchy.

Sultan Abdul Hamid I, who succeeded the throne after the death of his brother, Mustafa III, in 1774, was humiliated by the Ottoman Empire's recent defeats at the hands of Russia and believed that reforms were necessary to make sure the empire retained its status and glory. However, the new sultan only introduced new military equipment for the army and the navy. He was blind to the structural problems of his institutions. In addition, he saw great resistance from the *sipahi* and the Janissary corps when he tried to invite European commanders to become advisors to the military without requiring them to convert to Islam. While the *sipahis* and Janissaries saw this change as unholy and unneeded, the truth of the matter was that European tactics and strategies were far more advanced than anything the old-fashioned Ottoman army officials used at the time. And this lack of modernization greatly impacted the development of the state.

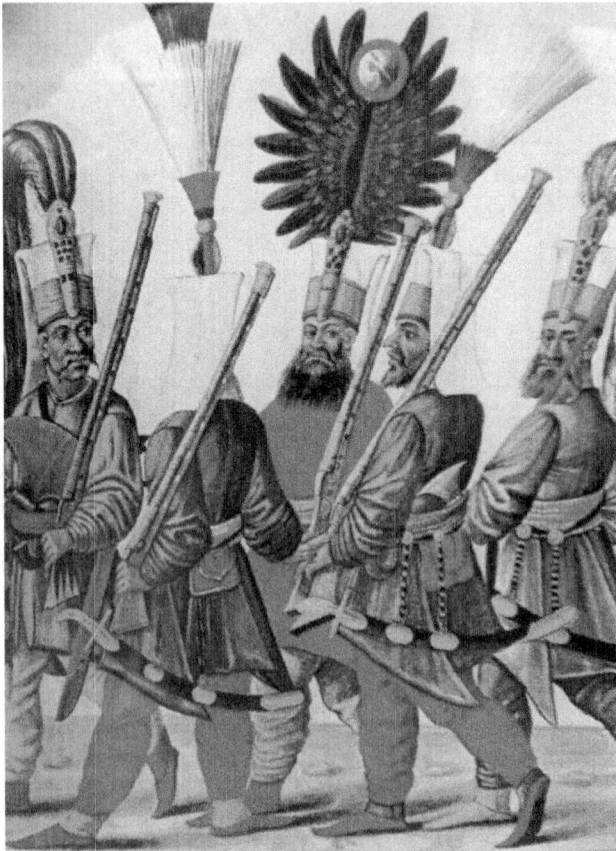

Ottoman Janissaries.
https://commons.wikimedia.org/wiki/File:Battle_of_Vienna.SultanMurads_with_janissaries .jpg

As the empire lost its foreign wars, it also declined internally. Due to the weakness of the central government, the landowners and the governors of different provinces started to operate largely on their own, fielding their own armies, raising their own taxes, and maintaining their own relations with their counterparts, something that greatly weakened the empire's integrity. It was as if the Ottoman system was becoming more and more feudal, especially in the Balkans, where most of the empire's Christian population resided. In the Balkans, the local rulers improved their standing and prestige now that Russia had become their "protector." The less supervised practice of religion and more autonomy eventually resulted in the rise of nationalist movements in many parts of the empire, as Serbs, Bosnians, Greeks, and other ethnic minorities increasingly demanded more rights. After the French Revolution, the concepts of nationalism and liberalism became more and more prominent throughout Europe. The cohesion of these movements within the borders of the Ottoman Empire greatly increased, posing a further threat to the sultan's position and the central government in Istanbul.

Many historians believe the disparity between the Ottoman and European societies when it came to social and technological aspects during the age of industrialization was caused mostly by the Ottomans' belief that they were, by nature, superior to their Christian counterparts. In addition, beginning in the days of the Protestant Reformation, the borders between the higher and lower ranks were slowly disappearing, allowing for members of different classes to become more familiarized with the customs of each other. However, the Ottoman high class was still largely confined to its own bubble, blind to the overall situation of the realm. This isolation of the Ottomans from the modern European structure of politics, economy, society, and military, which had proven to be much more effective, gave the Ottoman Empire a severe disadvantage.

Although one could argue that the Ottomans were at least on even terms with the Europeans culturally, the overall situation in the empire was far from what it had been during its golden age under Suleyman the Magnificent. The great artists, poets, scientists, artisans, and architects, who had enjoyed the sultans' protection and were admired among all people, no longer had such a glorious status. Some Ottoman grand viziers and sultans had tried to force Europeanization upon their subjects but failed in their efforts. For example, during the so-called Tulip Era, which lasted from 1718 to 1730, several members of the Ottoman high class tried to adopt some European standards and customs. They started to dress and look like their European counterparts, and the tulips they planted in their gardens and wore as parts of their outfits were symbols of nobility and status. However, unlike Russia, for example, another empire where efforts of Europeanization were taken to the extreme by rulers like Peter the Great and Catherine the Great, the Ottoman officials were simply not that interested in familiarizing themselves with what Europe stood for. Plus, due to strict divisions of the social strata, whatever changes the higher classes temporarily adopted rarely reached the rest of society.

Selim III

The man who would try to rescue the empire from its poisonous, old-fashioned roots was Sultan Selim III, who ascended the throne in 1789 and ruled until 1807. Starting his reign amidst the wars against Austria and Russia, which had renewed after short periods of peace, the first years of Selim III's reign proved to be just as difficult for the empire as the decades prior to them. Overwhelmed by Christian enemies, in 1792, the Ottomans sued for peace with both of their rivals, ceding complete control of the Caucasus and Crimea to the Russians and recognizing the Balkan territories (which the empire had retained, despite them being occupied by Austrian forces during the war) as protectorates of the Habsburg monarchy.

Selim III started his reign pretty disastrously, but the policies he would adopt later as sultan earned him his place in history. Selim correctly recognized the flaws of the Ottoman state and set out to introduce reforms that would address those problems. His agenda, which went by the name of Nizam-i-Cedid ("New Order"), was centered on the creation of a new army that would help the sultan restore control of the central government over the Ayans (the provincial governors and nobles). The sultan was challenged by the absence of modern equipment and suitable leaders, both of which were absolutely necessary for fielding a competent army.

Thus, Selim personally oversaw the creation of the Imperial School of Military Engineering, which was completed in 1795. He employed experienced French military personnel in the school. The newly arrived Europeans shared their knowledge when it came to modern warfare. In addition, the Ottoman upper classes, which had to increasingly spend time with the Europeans, learned more about their customs, societal and political structures, and values. This eventually led to the establishment of a permanent Ottoman diplomatic presence in European capitals, further connecting the two and aiding in the assimilation of the European way of life.

Nizam-i-Cedid was a rather costly project. Although it contributed to Ottoman modernization, it required a lot of funds the empire simply did not possess, as the economy had declined after the constant wars and the rise of colonial powers. Selim had to raise the tax rates, heavily taxing the Ayans. Then, he debased the coinage and imposed new taxes on various everyday goods like tobacco.

All of these changes imposed hardships on the population and, when paired with the fact that a completely new army was being created, caused a hostile reaction from the more traditional parties within the Ottoman society, namely the *sipahis*, the Janissaries, and members of the religious classes. These parties believed the sultan's changes turned away from the traditional Islamic Ottoman society. Thus, they challenged almost all of Selim's decisions. Eventually, believing that the new reforms posed a threat to their standing in the empire, they instigated an insurgence against the Crown and became the leading cause of the sultan's demise.

The resistance from within the empire was not the only force acting against the sultan. With the rise of nationalism and the birth of new nation-states in Europe after the French Revolution, multiethnic empires, such as the Ottoman Empire, faced the risk of dissolution. After the conquests of Napoleon, who from 1798 to 1801 invaded Mamluk-controlled Egypt, which had been under Ottoman suzerainty, nationalist sentiments rose high throughout the empire, posing a threat to the central government. Napoleon claimed he liberated the conquered nations throughout Europe and contributed greatly to the Balkan nations' increasing hostility against Istanbul. The Christian subjects of the Balkans had long been the targets of Russia and Austria for exploitation. Most notably, the Serbian Revolution, which began in 1804, proved to be very difficult for Selim to deal with, especially since it was followed by a war with Russia in 1806.

By the end of his reign in 1807, Selim's reforms had greatly affected most of Ottoman society, some to a better extent than others. His "Army of the New Order," comprised of highly disciplined, trained, and well-equipped men, was no less than twenty thousand strong, and the higher classes of the empire had moved closer toward becoming more modern and European. However, the financial decisions the sultan had made weakened the economy, and the upset Janissaries and *sipahis* led an insurrection against the sultan in 1807, afraid that Selim would eventually replace them with his new soldiers. In late May, they stormed the palace in Istanbul and forced the sultan to abdicate. Despite Selim's gruesome end, he is still regarded as one of the earliest sultans who tried to address the empire's problems with reforms.

Chapter 7: The Sick Man of Europe

By the turn of the 19th century, the Ottoman Empire had lost most of its former glory. When compared to the rest of Europe, the empire lagged behind in almost every aspect, with the dominant parties of the Ottoman elite refusing to adopt many of the social and political changes other European nations embraced, fearful that it would lead to the loss of their status and power. This reluctance would lead the empire into a tumultuous period. The Ottomans tried to struggle their way back to the top, albeit with limited success.

The final chapter of this book will talk about the last 120 years of the Ottoman Empire's existence, covering the crucial developments that led to its dissolution after World War I.

The Tolls of Nationalism

When Selim III was overthrown by the anti-reform forces in 1807, there was no doubt the empire's future was rather precarious. The 19th century would be the age of modernization in Europe, where advancements in technology, economics, and industry resulted in impactful changes in human thought and political culture, giving birth to ideas like liberalism, nationalism, and early versions of democracy. Modernization reduced the influence of great empires and monarchies throughout the continent, and some rulers were able to resist the changes better than others. All in all, conservative rulership was on the decline, something that was alarming for the social strata that had been in power for centuries.

The political chaos in Istanbul after the deposition of Selim III continued for nearly a year, during which time the rival parties all tried to take control of the power vacuum. Eventually, Mahmud II would emerge as the new sultan of the empire, thanks to the efforts of his more powerful and cunning allies in the court, especially Bayrakdar Mustafa Pasha, his grand vizier. However, the grand vizier would only last a few months, as his radical anti-conservative reforms led to another insurrection in November 1808. Having further reduced the power of the traditionally powerful forces within the empire and, in a way, continued what Selim III had started, especially after the Janissaries killed Bayrakdar Mustafa Pasha in their insurrection, in which they again stormed Istanbul.

Mahmud II retained power and managed to negotiate with the rebels. Crucially, he correctly recognized the reforms that were directed toward the reduction of the Janissaries' power would be useless since they had constantly undermined any changes in the army's traditional structure. In fact, Mahmud knew the Ottoman army needed modernization and understood that the Janissaries stood in his way of fielding a military worthy of his European counterparts. Thus, if reforming the Janissaries was impossible, the only possible way to improve the military would be to destroy their corps completely.

To confront the Janissaries, Mahmud had to deal with more immediate problems, most importantly the nationalist Balkan uprisings that had begun due to the instability in Istanbul.

The revolts in the Balkans were already well underway by the time Mahmud became sultan. The nationalist movement in Serbia, under Kara George, had started a revolt in 1804, but instead of strengthening the presence of the central government in Belgrade, Selim III had disbanded the garrisoned Janissaries. This only poured fuel to the Serbian nationalist fire, and for a time, it looked like the Serbs had a shot at independence, especially after Russia intervened on behalf of their Orthodox brothers. The Russians invaded Wallachia to weaken Ottoman control in the region.

In 1813, Mahmud II finally managed to consolidate his armies and brutally suppressed the rebellion but failed to address the main concerns of the upset Serbian populace. Two years later, during a new revolt under the leadership of Miloš Obrenović, the Serbians would negotiate with the central government in Istanbul, obtaining a special autonomous status but still remaining under the control of the empire.

The fighting spirit of the Serbs, as well as contemporary nationalist movements throughout the rest of Europe, led to another Balkan nation revolting against the central government in Istanbul. Since 1814, multiple secret societies had sprung up throughout the big cities of the Ottoman Empire in Anatolia and the Balkans with the goal of creating a united Greek independence movement. Most importantly, the Filiki Eteria ("Society of Friends"), which was supported and funded by many of the powerful Greek families of the empire, gained prominence and planned multiple rebellions throughout the Balkans that would undermine Ottoman control over the territories and lead to Greece's independence.

By 1821, plans were in place to rebel in Wallachia and Moldavia, the Morea, and even Istanbul. The rebellions, which were instigated by the Filiki Eteria, were launched in early 1821 but were mostly suppressed. In 1825, Mahmud II called for reinforcements from Ottoman-controlled Egypt, which arrived under Ibrahim Pasha and helped the sultan reestablish control over the Greek provinces. With the combined forces, the sultan was able to exploit the weakness of the rebels who had collapsed after their failure. The sultan seized Athens in 1826, swinging the tide back into the hands of the central government.

However, what would determine the course of the war would be the intervention of the European powers on the side of Greece. In 1827, realizing that the instability in the Balkans would further weaken the Ottoman Empire, Russia, France, and Great Britain all sent forces to help the Greeks put up a fight against the Ottomans. Their fleets, which arrived near the shores of the Morea in the summer of 1827, eventually confronted the Ottoman-Egyptian naval force near Navarino, where the two sides engaged in a massive naval battle on October 20th. The superior European forces were able to decisively defeat the Ottoman fleet, sinking more than fifty Muslim ships and causing the Ottoman garrisons all around Greece to surrender. The Ottomans had exhausted their resources and were eventually defeated.

According to the Treaty of Adrianople in 1829 between the Ottomans and the Russians, Greece was recognized as a fully autonomous region, which led to its recognition as a sovereign independent nation by Britain, Russia, and France in 1830 with the London Protocol. Two years later, in 1832, with the Treaty of Constantinople, the Ottoman government declared Greece an independent nation-state.

The Serbian and Greek rebellions were a clear sign of the dwindling Ottoman power. Nationalism was getting stronger each day, but the Ottomans could not find a sufficient answer to it. The concept of independent nation-states was deadly for large heterogenous empires like the Ottomans and led to territorial disintegration, as highlighted by the events of the 1820s.

Reforms of Mahmud II

Mahmud II waged war against the Serbs, the Greeks, and the European powers that came to their aid. He also waged war against the Janissary corps. By the time Greece had openly revolted, he had managed to severely undermine their influence. Surrounding himself with loyal servants and military officers, he fiercely answered back whenever the Janissaries tried to resist the changes the sultan planned to implement. In 1826, for example, thousands of Janissaries tried to revolt against the central government. The sultan brutally dealt with them by executing and imprisoning most of them during the events known as the "Auspicious Incident." These kinds of confrontations between the sultan and the opposing forces led Mahmud II to request aid from the Egyptians in the war against the Greeks. His armies were divided, and loyalists were busy fighting the Janissaries.

In 1831, Mahmud II abolished the age-old timar system, a move that caused the final dissolution of the Janissary corps. Timars, the lands that had been distributed to elite military members after conquering territories, had long been the main source of the Janissaries' power, as the Janissaries had managed to grow their revenue exponentially after centuries of wars. Thus, in 1831, when the forces loyal to the sultan seized the timars, they essentially destroyed the Janissary corps from the inside. The new army, which had been built up even more after the efforts of Selim, became a dependable force. Instead of relying on conquests to give servicemen pieces of land, the sultan paid the military salaries directly from the royal treasury. These changes caused a chain reaction and led to modernization and the need for reforms in other fields of life. Although the Ottoman Empire was still far from reaching European levels of progress, the government had at least made some efforts to catch up with the rest of the great powers.

The dissolution of the Janissary corps and the creation of a more professional, dependable army soon allowed Mahmud II to seize more power in Istanbul. In the age of nationalism, when the cries for freedom and liberalization rang throughout the world, one way for empires and monarchies to deal with the impending crisis was to create new channels of bureaucratic control. Mahmud II also reorganized the empire's governmental structure. He created new administrative institutions, which helped him distribute the power and divide the responsibilities that were previously assumed by the grand vizier. Mahmud continued to open embassies and sent representatives to different European nations, something that led to further developments in society, as the dignitaries introduced European social, political, and economic systems to the Ottomans back home.

Due to the new systems and a much better army, Mahmud II was able to somewhat restore the power of the central government in Istanbul. The local governors and lords that had posed a threat to Ottoman control were dealt with in Rumelia and Anatolia. The only place where the sultan's efforts were rendered useless was Egypt, whose ruler, Muhammad Ali, rose up in an open rebellion in 1831 and invaded Syria, defeating the Ottoman forces at the Battle of Konya. For another nine years, the Ottomans struggled to reassert their dominance over the Egyptians, but with the Treaty in London in 1840, Muhammad Ali was recognized as the ruler of Egypt, although some lost territories were returned to Istanbul.

The Tanzimat

Mahmud II's reign marks a radical change in the overall Ottoman approach to the political and socioeconomic life of the empire. Unlike other figures who had tried to introduce reforms before him, Sultan Mahmud II was devoted to Europeanizing his realm and believed the only possible way to achieve his goal was to move away from the traditional Ottoman institutions. By the end of his reign in 1839, the sultan had pushed his mindset onto his subjects, something that would be clearly demonstrated for another thirty or so years, as Mahmud's successors continued to implement changes that would contribute to the empire's development.

In Ottoman history, the reigns of Sultan Abdülmecid I (r. 1839–1861) and Abdülaziz (r. 1861–1876) have come to be known as the Tanzimat ("Reorganization") era. As previously mentioned, the Tanzimat saw the introduction of major changes in the administrative and social life of the Ottoman Empire, which greatly influenced developments within the realm. The Tanzimat began in November 1839 when Sultan Abdülmecid I assembled the most important members of his court, as well as local and foreign officials, in the rose garden of Topkapi Palace in Istanbul. There, he issued a new royal decree by the name of *Hatt-ı Şerif of Gülhane*—the Noble Edict of the Rose Garden.

The decree included many vital points and would forever change life in the Ottoman Empire. Mainly, it made the central government responsible for carrying out the decree and committed the empire to a series of important reforms, including the implementation of new legal systems, fighting corruption in the administration, and a complete overhaul of the taxation system. It demonstrated the sultan's wish to make the law the most respected entity within the empire and promised just treatment to all subjects, regardless of their status, religion, or ethnicity. Through the decree, the central government was bound to address the issues the document pointed out, and for more than three decades, it would systematically try to implement new changes in all aspects of life.

The decree diverted from the traditional Ottoman system, in which the empire only had a vague responsibility of defending its subjects. The decree significantly expanded the government's responsibilities toward everyone who lived within its borders, something that was borrowed from 19th-century Europe. Defending the people from foreign threats was not enough. The Ottomans in charge realized they had to serve their people for the people to serve them back.

The government was divided into different bureaucratic institutions, with different teams of officials working on the implementation of different changes. A highly centralized administrative system needed good communications and infrastructural systems. Thus, one of the most important developments the Tanzimat brought about was building connecting roads between the various population centers of the empire, mainly in Anatolia and the Balkans. In addition to roads, railway and telegraph lines were built, with their centers at Istanbul, making it easier for the central government to transfer resources and information throughout the empire. Increased connectivity also meant a boost to the Ottoman economy, which benefited greatly from the new infrastructural projects.

A major part of the Tanzimat was the significant improvement of the Ottoman education system, which, just like other aspects of Ottoman life, lagged behind the rest of Europe. Some of the previous sultans had promoted educational reforms, building new universities and colleges that specialized in different areas. Throughout the reformatory period, new institutions were founded, including the civil service school in 1859, whose graduates were educated in governance and administration.

However, the main obstacle was that the Muslim millets (small administrative divisions) still gave a strictly Islamic education to the majority of the young population. With the introduction of the rushdiye schools (the first public education institutions in the Ottoman Empire), the government provided the adolescent graduates of the millets with a secular education, building on the traditional Islamic values taught to them in their youth and educating them in a way to make them fit for the modern world. Despite the fact the millets did not teach the youth humanities or modern sciences, blatantly going against the millets would upset the Muslim *ulama*, which still was an influential actor in the empire, and produce a conflict between the government and the religious officials.

In 1846, a completely new system of primary and secondary schools was introduced, combining the traditional and modern elements of education and contributing to the creation of a cohesive educational system. After completing these steps, the youngsters were encouraged to attend one of the empire's universities based on their interests and skills. All in all, the Tanzimat essentially created a base of much-needed secular educational opportunities in the Ottoman Empire, providing education to hundreds of thousands of Ottoman youngsters.

The Tanzimat also greatly changed the financial and legal systems of the Ottoman Empire. The appointed bureaucrats were now responsible for tax collection, and the process was simplified. Legal reforms were also directed to the modernization (but not complete abandonment) of the Islamic Sharia, which had served as one of the empire's foundations. Many new codes were drafted and issued during the three decades of the Tanzimat, providing a basis for the inception of the first written constitution of the Ottoman Empire in the mid-1870s. Borrowing heavily from the French and British legal systems, these changes were largely based on improving the overall quality of life for all Ottoman subjects.

Despite the relative success of the Tanzimat, the period from the late 1830s to the mid-1870s was by no means easy for the Ottoman Empire, as it not only found itself in a series of wars against its subjects and foreign powers but also met domestic resistance from conservative actors. The underlying problem of the reorganization era was the lack of funds, as the reforms needed a lot of money. The implemented reforms contributed to economic growth, but whatever short-term gains the Crown saw, it would often reinvest the money to implement other changes.

Internal rebellions and wars also posed severe problems to the empire's integrity. In addition to the war with Egypt's Muhammad Ali, which resulted in Egyptian autonomy in early 1841, Ottoman suzerainty was further challenged in the Balkans, where the Russian-promoted Pan-Slavic ideology saw a revival. Motivated by the recent successes of the Greek and, to a lesser extent, Serbian nationalist movements, revolts broke out in Bosnia and Montenegro many times, with the rebels getting assistance from Serbia and Russia. Although Ottoman power was eventually restored in the rebelling nations of the Balkans by the mid-1870s, the Crown had to make significant concessions to its minorities, including even more autonomous rights. By the end of the Tanzimat, although the Christian regions of the empire were still technically under the central government's control, they largely acted as fully independent nations, exploiting the Crown's limited authority in their territories.

The Ottoman Empire also found itself in yet another war with Russia, which erupted in 1853 over Crimea. Seeing itself as a champion of Orthodoxy, Russia had long pursued a rather cunning foreign policy of supporting the Orthodox minorities in the Balkans, who had always posed a threat to the Ottoman government. The tensions between the two sides reached their peak when the Ottomans supported Catholic claims over the rights of the holy sites in Jerusalem. Russia supported the Orthodox peoples and opposed Rome. Thus, Nicholas I of Russia invaded Ottoman-controlled Wallachia and Moldavia, but the Ottomans were able to defeat the Russians with the help of the Europeans, namely the French and the British, who sent their fleets to the Black Sea to deescalate the situation.

Although the Ottomans suffered a big naval defeat against the Russians at the Battle of Sinope in November 1853, their joint military campaigns with the French and the British eventually led to the fall of Sevastopol, forcing Russia to sue for peace. Still, despite achieving victory in the war, the Ottoman Empire did not see any immediate benefits, though Russia's position was weakened in the contested regions and the Black Sea.

The Reaction to the Tanzimat

Despite the measures that were taken during the Tanzimat, the Ottoman Empire entered a very difficult period of instability in the latter half of the 1870s. The empire's financial troubles truly showed themselves throughout the 1870s, as a series of unfortunate events caused mass discontent. First of all, to keep up with the reforms and encourage economic growth and training of new bureaucratic personnel, the Ottoman Empire found itself in great debt. Wars against the rebelling provinces throughout the 1850s and 1860s only caused more financial difficulties, while the Crimean War did not result in significant gains for the Ottoman Empire. Thus, the Crown had to take out multiple foreign loans worth millions of pounds. The debt and the unfavorable climate conditions of 1873 and 1874 upset the population even more.

In addition, the recently suppressed Balkan revolts had still not ceased in spirit, and the empire entered another war with Russia in

1877 over the status of its Christian subjects in the Balkans. The main Ottoman force was defeated at the Battle of Plevna in late 1877, forcing Istanbul to sue for peace. The Treaty of San Stefano, signed in March of 1878 between the Ottomans and Russians, forced the Ottoman Empire to give up significant control over its Balkan holdings and recognize the autonomy of Bulgaria and the independence of Serbia, Montenegro, and Romania. Russia regained control of the contested territories in eastern Anatolia, including Kars, Batum, and Ardahan. Although the treaty would be revised in the Berlin Conference in June of the same year with minor territorial tweaks, the Ottoman Empire was still significantly weakened by the outcome, losing control of about 8 percent of its total territories and 4.5 million subjects. Bulgaria, which remained under nominal Ottoman control, was largely a Russian satellite. Austria occupied and administered Bosnia. Romania, Montenegro, and Serbia, which were now independent nations, gained new territories, and Britain assumed control of the island of Cyprus.

After the Berlin Conference, the Ottoman European territories were reduced to Thrace, Macedonia, and parts of Albania, and the empire's holdings were surrounded by hostile parties on all sides. The Europeans also came to collect their money from the Ottomans, leading to the creation of the Ottoman Public Debt Administration (OPDA), which reduced the overall debt but still could not sufficiently address the empire's economic problems. Throughout the years, as foreign influence on Istanbul increased, the OPDA acted as more than an entity to control the public debt. Instead, it started to mediate relations between European financial institutions seeking to invest in the Ottoman Empire, becoming an influential institution itself.

In parallel to the Ottoman struggles in foreign and domestic wars, the empire saw a great expansion of political culture throughout the 1870s, something that can partially be attributed to the developments in education. As more and more Ottoman youths received a modern education and traveled and experienced life in other European countries, the more they started gathering and sharing their ideas with each other, eventually forming societies where they could express their political views. The Young Ottomans emerged as the most prominent organization, uniting individuals with different innate beliefs and becoming one of the first Turkish nationalist movements in history. Led by Namik Kemal, the Young Ottomans wished for the creation of a constitutional monarchy where the sultan's powers would be limited and checked by the institutions outlined in the Constitution. Although they expressed their desire for modernization and their admiration of Europe, the Young Ottomans did not favor the reforms of the Tanzimat, believing them to be too radically Western in thought. They did not want to abandon the empire's traditional Islamic roots.

Ironically, as the Young Ottomans gained more followers and expanded their political culture, they were greatly aided by the changes of the Tanzimat, which allowed for more facilitated means of transmitting information. The Tanzimat helped to create newspapers, develop infrastructure, and increase freedoms. Thus, by 1876, when the empire found itself in a period of crisis, the views of the Young Ottomans were largely shared by members of the court and the administration. With the installment of Sultan Abdul Hamid II in 1876 after a brief succession dilemma, the new cabinet of ministers, led by Midhat Pasha, pushed for the implementation of more conservative reforms, including the issue of a constitution.

The Ottoman Constitution, which was signed and issued in December 1876, was one of the first constitutions in the Islamic world. However, although its premise had been the creation of a constitutional monarchy, where the power of the sovereign would be limited by other institutions, the Ottoman Constitution instead declared the supreme authority of the sultan, which it also referred to as the "Kaliph and the supreme protector of all of the Muslim world." The sultan retained his full executive powers and was able to appoint his ministers and staff. In regard to legislation, a bicameral parliament was implemented, consisting of the Senate (appointed by the sultan) and the Chamber of Deputies (the representatives would be elected every four years). Thus, the Ottoman Constitution of 1876 did not really strip the sultan of his powers, but it did point out the duties of the new parliament.

All in all, the Constitution, as well as the rule of Abdul Hamid II, is largely considered a reaction to the Tanzimat era that preceded them. The reforms of the Tanzimat, which were considered too

Western by the Young Ottomans and many of the officials of the empire, were followed up by the Ottoman Constitution, which failed to strip power away from the sultan but nevertheless laid a foundation for the creation of a constitutional monarchy.

The Young Turk Revolution

Perhaps the Ottoman Constitution of 1876 did not quite achieve what it had hoped for, as the empire was still far from becoming a well-functioning constitutional monarchy. However, Sultan Abdul Hamid II's reign, which started with the declaration of the Constitution, should not be regarded as a period of further decline. Unlike some of his predecessors who had failed to competently lead the realm due to their personal strife and reluctance to adopt changes, Abdul Hamid II managed to somewhat consolidate the empire's position. As a sultan with virtually unlimited power, he made an effort to preserve the territorial integrity of the Ottoman Empire after decades of internal instability had led to the independence of its Balkan holdings.

In fact, Abdul Hamid II's reign saw some improvements in the realm. Continuing the practice of military conscription, which had been started during the Tanzimat, Abdul Hamid invested a lot in further modernizing the Ottoman army. He tried to purchase military equipment from European powers since he lacked the means to produce them in the empire. Aided in his endeavors by his trusted grand vizier, Mehmed Said Pasha, the sultan wished to hold absolute power over his subjects and created a complex spy network and a new police force to keep order. The Ottoman Constitution declared him the supreme protector of all Muslims, motivating him to fund projects that would cement his position as the caliph. Due to the development of regional infrastructure, the sultan was able to increase connectivity in the predominantly Muslim part of his realm, constructing telegraph and railway lines in southeastern Anatolia, Syria, and Palestine and connecting Damascus to Medina with the crucial Hejaz Railway, which was completed in 1908.

Still, the sultan was rather unpopular among the more liberal-minded Ottomans, who believed he often overused his powers to gain favors from the Muslim population while negatively impacting his other subjects. The fact he had disbanded the parliament not even a year after its introduction and never recalled it until was certainly a major concern. To them, this act was clearly undemocratic and went against the Constitution.

These individuals also protested the brutal repression of the Armenian population. Although the Armenians had been loyal Christian subjects to the empire, at least for the most part (unlike the Balkan minorities who had rebelled on many occasions), after assuming power, Abdul Hamid II started to increasingly strip them of their lands and encouraged Muslim emigration. Hundreds of thousands of Armenians were forced to leave their homes in eastern Anatolia and move farther east, resulting in the creation of nationalist movements that wished to resist suppression. Not only that, but beginning in 1891, the sultan created special Muslim police forces that brutally persecuted Armenians throughout eastern Anatolia and the South Caucasus.

The persecution of Armenians coincided with the loss of Ottoman territories in North Africa, which further increased anti-sultan sentiments in the more educated spheres of the population. In 1881 and 1882, the Ottoman Empire lost its influence in Tunis and Egypt to the French and the British, respectively. These parts of the realm already functioned as largely autonomous regions, although they were technically still under Ottoman suzerainty. However, the Europeans had long perceived them as their spheres of influence and proceeded to occupy them in the first half of the 1880s. Although these territories would formally be under Ottoman control until World War One, the occupation of Egypt and Tunis by British and French forces signaled the sultan's weakness.

Thus, since the early years of Abdul Hamid II's reign, the number of individuals who disliked the sultan increased heavily, assembling as underground societies and planning multiple conspiracies against him. There was the Committee of Union and Progress (CUP), which regarded itself as the successor of the Young Ottomans and was commonly referred to as the "Young Turks." The CUP was the most prominent Turkish nationalist movement, having many supporters not only in the empire but also outside its borders, such as France. The Young Turks frequently met cities like Paris, where they discussed their ideas regarding their country and published several newspapers where they expressed their concerns. Although some of the factions of the Young Turks clashed ideologically, especially when it came to European involvement in Ottoman affairs, the main thinkers of the group all agreed the Ottoman Empire had to be significantly reformed. They believed the sultan possessed too much power and authority, which was not up to standards with the rest of the developed world. Led by prominent liberal and conservative Ottoman exiles, the Young Turks slowly consolidated their power and gained enough traction with ordinary citizens and among the members of the higher ranks.

Eventually, in 1908, the Young Turks emerged as forebearers of a revolution, toppling Abdul Hamid II's regime and establishing a constitutional monarchy in its place after months of political processes. However, the CUP did not instigate a rebellion or storm Topkapi Palace to depose the sultan. Instead, the Young Turks found the spark of revolution among the members of the Ottoman Third Army, which was at the time stationed in Macedonia. In the early summer of 1908, led by Major Ahmed Niyazi and later joined by officer Ismail Enver, most of the army mutinied, scattering around the region and organizing themselves into guerilla bands. They defeated any forces the sultan sent to suppress him. The reason behind their mutiny is not exactly clear, but most historians believe that difficult conditions and harsh treatment of the army caused the men to rise up against the sultan.

Soon, the Third Army managed to take control of the city of Edirne and came dangerously close to Istanbul. Their numbers grew day by day, with people joining from different parts of the empire. By July 24th, Sultan Abdul Hamid II realized he could no longer overpower the revolutionaries and, fearing deposition, gave in to their demands.

Declaration of the 1908 Young Turk Revolution.
https://commons.wikimedia.org/wiki/File:Declaration_of_the_1908_Revolution_in_Ottom
an_Empire.png

The exact relationship between the CUP and the leaders of the Third Army has not been determined, although it is known that many mutineers held similar anti-monarchy views, believing that Abdul Hamid's regime would only lead to the empire's further demise. Their beliefs were mostly reinforced by the constant loss of Ottoman power and influence in different regions throughout the realm. Still, their main demand was the restoration of the Ottoman Constitution of 1876, with which the sultan agreed. However, when the bicameral parliament structure was reinstated, it soon became clear the revolutionaries did not quite know what to do after gaining power. They had no plans for the government's formation. The Ottoman Senate convened for the first time in over three decades in December 1908 after liberal Kamil Pasha's election as the new grand vizier. Many political parties comprised of members of the lower classes were created and ran for election for the Chamber of Deputies, which would first convene in January 1909.

The Second Constitutional Era

Thus started the so-called Second Constitutional Era of the Ottoman Empire, which would last until the empire's collapse in 1922. With the parliament restored and the sultan's powers greatly reduced, Abdul Hamid tried to rally his supporters once again to try and resist the Young Turks. Despite an array of promises, like restoring the great Islamic caliphate and returning to the Sharia legal system, Abdul Hamid's efforts were in vain. In April 1909, in the events of the "31ˢᵗ March Incident" (named after the old Julian calendar), parts of the army that supported the sultan's claims revolted against the Young Turk government and tried to seize power. However, in just eleven days, the central government was able to restore order. The mutineers were imprisoned, and Abdul Hamid II was finally deposed. Mehmed V replaced him as the new sultan.

Although the CUP had restored order in the empire, the government was still largely disorganized. The Young Turks were, in all regards, young and inexperienced when it came to ruling such a vast empire that was undergoing a period of decline. Despite their promises and hopes to save the Ottoman Empire from utter collapse, nothing really changed. In the elections of 1912, the CUP again won the majority in the parliament, but their success was overshadowed by the Ottoman Empire's defeat against Italy over the Libyan North African coast. The Italians smashed the Ottoman army, which, despite being heavily modernized, was not on Italy's level.

It has to be said that the CUP tried to avoid armed conflict in times of crisis and offered the Italians de facto control of the region, similar to the situation in Egypt (which was nominally still an Ottoman territory but was under British occupation). Nevertheless, the situation escalated in September 1911 and ended in a decisive Italian victory, something that humiliated the new government of Istanbul and acted as a precursor to another year of instability in the capital.

The loss of territory against the Italians was not the only foreign policy problem for the Ottomans. In 1908, Austria-Hungary proceeded with the annexation of Bosnia and Herzegovina, which were still technically under Ottoman control. In the same month, Bulgaria, backed by the Russian Empire, declared its independence from the Ottomans, almost completely driving the Turks out of southeastern Europe. The Young Turk government could not sufficiently react to these problems that threatened the empire's territorial integrity, as both conflicts coincided with the power struggle in the empire.

The latter half of 1912 saw the Ottomans in yet another war, this time with the coalition of newly formed Balkan states—Greece, Bulgaria, Serbia, and Montenegro. These nations had formed the Balkan League through a series of secret and public negotiations. In October 1912, just as the Ottoman war with Italy was coming to a close, the members of the alliance declared war on the empire one by one. By the end of the year, they managed to decisively defeat the Ottoman forces in the Balkans. After achieving multiple victories on land and in the sea, the Balkan League forced the Ottomans all the way back to Istanbul, at which point the Ottomans sued for peace and ceded large territories to the enemy nations.

In a few months, the members of the Balkan League went to war with each other, but the Ottoman Empire was unable to exploit the chaos in the region and sided with Bulgaria, eventually suffering defeat once again. It was unable to regain the lost territories. After a year of conflict, the peace negotiations came to a close in late 1913, and the Ottoman Empire lost almost all of its European lands, including Macedonia and Albania. The empire only retained control over a small part of southern Thrace, which included the city of Edirne.

In June 1913, the CUP finally consolidated its power after the assassination of the opposition leader, Shevket Pasha, and began to implement some of the changes it saw necessary for the empire's further modernization. The administrative reform of 1913 touched upon the provincial divisions within the empire, and with the new system, the Young Turks were able to raise more money through taxes. The government also tried to modernize the law; it did not completely abandon the Sharia but introduced new codes the ancient Islamic law did not address in much detail. The Young Turks promoted development and industrialization, which helped give the economy a slight boost. Construction of several new factories in Anatolia started in the Second Constitutional Era. In addition, the liberal government also pushed for more liberalization of the empire's social and political culture, promoting more freedom of speech and encouraging the creation of newspapers and other sources of media.

The Great War

Thus, by the time World War I began between the Central Powers and the Allies, a conflict that would shape the history of the world forever, the Young Turk government of the Ottoman Empire had at least tried to catch up with the rest of the modern world. Despite making some progress when it came to internal reforms, the Young Turks did not transform the Ottoman Empire from top to bottom as they had originally wished. The foreign policy catastrophes of the Young Turks had increased the Turkish nationalist sentiment throughout the empire, which was becoming more and more homogenous since more and more ethnic minorities escaped its suzerainty. Other great European powers often referred to the Ottoman Empire as the "sick man of Europe," pointing out the fact that it was a dying empire, unable to keep up with modern times.

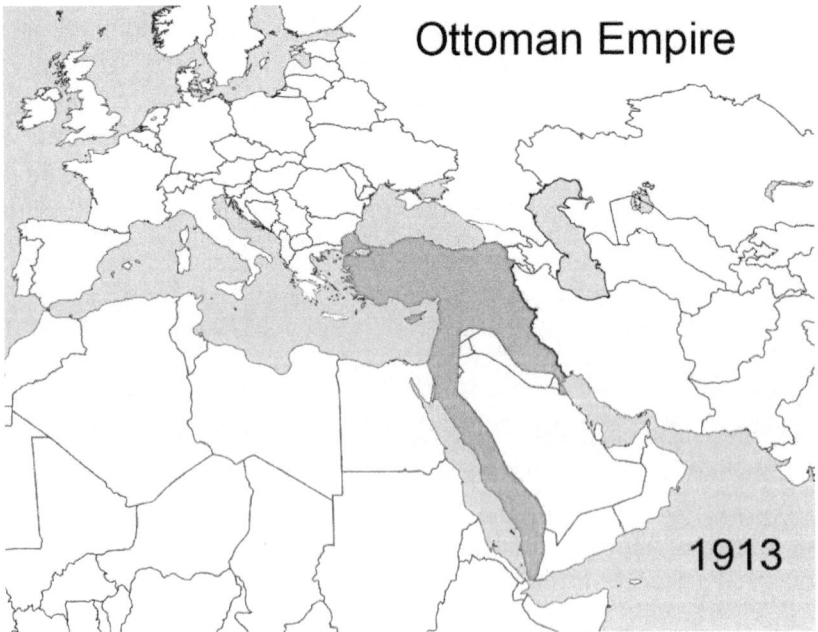

Ottoman Empire before the start of WWI.

The Ottoman Empire's defeats and the loss of so many territories before 1914 played a big role in the government's decision to eventually enter World War I in October 1914. Unlike other belligerents, the Ottomans had not been involved in the conflict since the very beginning (the war began in the summer of 1914. The empire had avoided being part of the complex systems of alliances that bound the European nations together, forcing them to aid each other in times of war. However, just like during the Second Balkan War, the Ottoman Empire wrongfully chose its allies, entering the war on the side of Germany and Austria-Hungary.

There are multiple reasons behind this decision. Historians mainly point to the German influence on the Ottoman government, which is thought to have ultimately decided the Ottomans' entry on the side of the Central Powers. Germany, which was perhaps the strongest faction in WWI alongside Britain, had been a supporter of the Young Turk government. Germany had not only financed many of the Ottoman Empire's infrastructural projects but also sent German officers to train the Ottoman military according to European standards. Additionally, at the beginning of the war, the Germans embarked on relatively successful offensives on the Western Front. It looked like the Central Powers would emerge victorious from the conflict very quickly, something that was eventually proven wrong since Germany and its allies were defeated after four years of bloody fighting.

However, back in 1914, the Ottoman high command, led by Minister of War Ismail Enver Pasha (the same Ismail Enver who mutinied in 1908), believed that joining the war on the side of the Central Powers would result in the recovery of the territories lost in the Balkans. So, on October 29th, 1914, the Ottoman high command ordered the bombardment of Russian port cities in the Black Sea, leading to the declaration of war.

To the surprise of many, the Ottoman Empire significantly contributed to the war effort, defending its territories on many different fronts against the forces of Britain, Russia, and France. After the deadlocked stalemate had been established on the Western Front, the Ottomans managed to successfully repel the Allied invasion of Gallipoli, one of the biggest Central Power victories of the war. Although the Ottoman Empire suffered some minor losses, it largely defeated the Russians in the Caucasus and stopped the British offensives in the Middle East, thanks to financial support from Germany. A bloody stain on the Ottoman Empire's legacy would be the brutal suppression of the Armenian population throughout the course of the war, as the Ottoman troops massacred more than a million Armenians in what has been dubbed the Armenian genocide. Encouraged by the rising Turkish nationalism, the Ottoman Empire's oppression of minorities remains one of the most horrible acts of WWI.

Despite their successes on the battlefield, the Ottomans fell prey to the problems that came with waging a long war. After the initial stalemate, the Central Powers found it difficult to break through the Allied trench lines, so no significant progress was made. On the Eastern Front, partially thanks to Ottoman efforts and the Russian Revolution, Russia had been forced to sign a separate peace treaty, but it was still not enough to achieve victory. Italy and the United States eventually joined the war on the side of the Allies, providing enough resources to help overwhelm the Central Powers.

Throughout all this time, the Ottoman population experienced rough living conditions, as the war effort caused severe economic problems. People were upset with the government, which, despite largely defending its territories, had failed to grasp victory in the war. As the Allies closed in on the Central Powers, the situation became desperate. With the fall of Bulgaria in late September 1918, the Young Turk government was forced to realize the war was lost, resigning on October 7th. A new government was formed under Ahmed Izzet Pasha two days later, and the Allied troops occupied the capital. By the end of the month, the Ottomans agreed to the Armistice of Mudros, ending their involvement in WWI.

Dissolution of the Empire and The Emergence of Turkey

The defeated Ottoman Empire was partitioned by the victorious Allied nations, with parts of it occupied by France, Britain, Italy, and Greece. However, the final terms of peace, which would result in the loss of most of the empire's territory, would not be presented by the Allies until August 1920. The Treaty of Sèvres reduced the Ottoman Empire's holdings to only parts of Anatolia. The empire's Middle Eastern provinces were divided by Britain and France, while Greece possessed the remainder of its European territories. Greece also controlled Smyrna and the land surrounding it, while Italy occupied the southern Anatolian coast. The newly created sovereign state of Armenia gained control of some of eastern Anatolia, including the cities of Trebizond and Erzurum. In the eyes of many, the Ottomans had been humiliated the most out of the defeated major powers.

The humiliating partition of the empire amplified the Turkish nationalist voices, which protested such a vile division of the Ottoman lands and believed it to have been an intrusion of Ottoman sovereignty by the victorious nations. Among the most vocal leaders of the Turkish nationalists was Mustafa Kemal Pasha, an Ottoman officer who had distinguished himself for his bravery in different campaigns throughout the war. After the empire's occupation by the Allies and before the official partition in 1920, he had been made the inspector general of the Ottoman forces in Anatolia and had gained even more prominence. In May 1919, Mustafa Kemal organized the nationalist-minded protesters in a united movement and, throughout the course of the summer, worked to establish the Turkish National Congress. His aim was to create a sort of counter-voice to the Ottoman government in occupied Istanbul, which he deemed unworthy of being in power. The Turkish National Congress assembled twice by the end of the year, first in Erzurum and then in Sivas, where it discussed its plans and visions for Turkish liberation from the occupying forces.

This was followed by the call for new parliamentary elections in Istanbul in January 1920 and the subsequent issue of the National Pact, a document that essentially officialized the demands of the nationalists. The pact demanded the recognition of all of Anatolia as a principal Ottoman territory and wanted the Allies to cease its occupation. In April, after the British forces that occupied Istanbul had replaced the grand vizier and tried to fight the nationalist, anti-foreign movements in the empire, the Grand National Assembly was convened in the city of Ankara, where many of the politicians had defected to escape the occupation of the capital.

The nationalist assembly elected Mustafa Kemal Pasha (later granted the nickname of Atatürk, "Father of the Turks) as its president. To make sure the royalist majority of Anatolia would support them, they declared that the president and the Congress would act on behalf of the sultan until he was freed from Allied occupation in Istanbul. At this point, the Grand National Assembly was still technically a quasi-governmental structure that opposed the central government in Istanbul, but it had managed to gain so many followers that it could effectively resist the other major forces within the empire. After declaring the two historical rivals of the Ottomans—Greece in the west and Armenia in the east—as the main threat to the security of the state, Mustafa Kemal Pasha organized a new army corps under the leadership of Ismet Pasha and tasked it with retrieving the lost territories under the control of these two nations.

In October, the nationalist forces moved east, capturing the cities of Ardahan and Kars from the Armenians and forcing them to sign the Treaty of Gümrü (also known as the Treaty of Alexandropol) in December, which changed up the borders between the two countries and ceded back much of the lost territories to the Ottomans. The Turkish nationalist drive was quickly recognized by the newly formed Soviet Union, which invaded and annexed the Caucasian nations of Georgia, Azerbaijan, and Armenia. The Soviet Union shared the anti-European stance of the nationalist movement and sought to drive the Allied forces as far away from its territories as possible.

Thus, in March 1921, Mustafa Kemal Pasha agreed to sign a treaty of friendship with the Soviet government, fixing the borders between the two states. The treaty also provided Mustafa Kemal Pasha with much-needed support to continue the war effort. This was followed by the recovery of the French-occupied territories in southeastern Anatolia in the historical region of Cilicia. The French, who were determined to establish control and continue the occupation of their gains in Syria, were uninterested in contesting the Turkish nationalists over Cilicia and agreed to give up the region in October 1921.

Then, Mustafa Kemal Pasha turned toward the west, where the Ottoman territories had been under constant threat from Greece. Having established control of the cities of Izmir and Bursa in western Anatolia, Greece was confident in its ability to permanently gain the occupied lands. For more than a year after the summer of 1921, the Turkish nationalists defended the western Anatolian lands from Greek attacks, managing to not only retain control of Ankara but also recover Bursa and Izmir. By September 1922, the Ottoman troops under Mustafa Kemal Pasha had destroyed the Greek forces at every instance and forced the Greeks to evacuate all of Anatolia. Fighting between the two nations ceased a month later after the British convinced the Greeks to abandon their offensives in Thrace and mediated the Armistice of Mudanya.

With nearly all of Anatolia recovered through the efforts of the Grand National Assembly, the British, who still occupied Istanbul, realized that it was time to finally end the hostilities in the region, which had persisted since the end of the war. Thus, in late October, they invited members of the central government in Istanbul to join peace talks in the Swiss city of Lausanne. However, the Grand National Assembly was not about to let the central government take all the credit for driving the occupiers out of the country's borders. On November 1st, it declared the sultan in Istanbul was no longer the head of the Turkish nation. Instead, Ismet Pasha, the nationalist officer from the Grand National Assembly, arrived in Lausanne in late November to represent the country.

Map of the Republic of Turkey after the Treaty of Lausanne
https://commons.wikimedia.org/wiki/File:Turkey-Greece-Bulgaria_on_Treaty_of_Lausanne.png

The Treaty of Lausanne, which was signed after months of negotiations in July 1923, is often considered to be the final treaty of World War I. It was signed nearly five years after the agreement of an armistice between the Allies and the Central Powers. In the document, both parties were forced to make significant concessions. According to the document, the Turkish government renounced its claims on its former Middle Eastern regions, the island of Cyprus, and some of the islands in the Mediterranean. In addition, it agreed to recognize the rights of all minorities within its borders, regardless of their ethnicity and religion, as well as accept international control over the Dardanelles and the Bosphorus. In return, it retained the territorial integrity of Anatolia and the control of Istanbul and its surrounding southern Thracian lands.

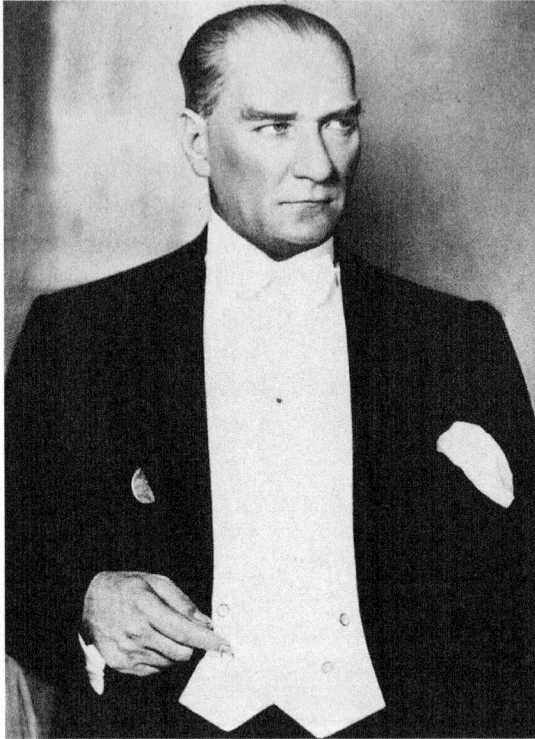

Mustafa Kemal Atatürk, the president of the Republic of Turkey, in 1932.
https://commons.wikimedia.org/wiki/File:Ataturk1930s.jpg

The Turkish delegation returned from Lausanne, and the two sides got around to complying with the terms of the treaty. The last British forces left Istanbul in the autumn of 1923 and embarked on a long journey home. The Grand National Assembly then turned its attention to the royal family, which it rightfully accused of conspiring with the foreigners in order to retain its position of power within the realm. The Grand National Assembly urged Sultan Abdulmejid II, who had nominally been in power since 1922, to leave the country. The assembly abolished the sultanate and sent the members of the royal family into exile.

In October 1923, the Grand National Assembly formally proclaimed the formation of the Republic of Turkey, with Mustafa Kemal as its first president. The capital was moved from Istanbul to Ankara. The year 1923 marked the final year of the Ottoman Empire's existence. For the next few decades, the Turkish government under President Atatürk would start the process of developing the newborn republic.

The once-mighty Ottoman Empire was thus succeeded by a democratic republic after more than six hundred years of existence.

Conclusion

The history of the Ottoman Empire is intriguing to study for any interested person, be it a casual history lover or a learned scholar. With its roots in Muslim Turkoman holy wars and expansion for dominance in the region, the empire soon emerged to be the most powerful state in Europe by the 16th century. Spanning a vast territory from Budapest to Constantinople to Baghdad to Jerusalem to Cairo to Tunis at the peak of its power, the Ottoman Empire remains one of the most powerful empires to have ever existed in medieval Europe, and the fact that it managed to last for over six hundred years is proof of that fact.

Starting from a small Turkish principality in northwestern Anatolia, Osman and his successors managed to create a realm like no other, dominating their rivals all around the world. Osman's successors would greatly contribute to the gradual decline and eventual dissolution of the empire in the 20th century. As the Ottomans forged their identity in conquest and war, they neglected the crucial developments of the early modern era, which resulted in the lack of modernization and hindered the empire's further advancement. The Ottoman sultans were not the only rulers who fell prey to the hardships that are innate to controlling such a vast and diverse empire. The Habsburgs and the Romanovs—two of the rival monarchies of the Ottomans—also failed to adapt to the developments in political thought and culture, which led to their similar demise.

It is very interesting to think about what would have happened if things had gone differently for the Ottomans, who had a greater head start when it came to overall strength compared to their European counterparts. Not only did the Ottoman Empire field the largest and strongest army in the known world, but it was also one of the most technologically, culturally, and socially advanced societies. Life thrived within the great cities of the empire, with people from different backgrounds coexisting. However, from the 17th century onward, many external and domestic factors contributed to the empire's collapse, the least of which was the overall weakness of the empire's sultans.

Nevertheless, it is both the highs and the lows of the Ottoman Empire that make it very interesting to study. The aim of this book was to present the main timeline from the formation of the empire from its Anatolian roots to its eventual dissolution after World War I. The history of the Ottoman Empire remains compelling and enthralling for many reasons, and the empire has certainly left behind one of the greatest legacies. It will forever be remembered in the history books.

Part 2: Suleiman the Magnificent

An Enthralling Guide to the Sultan Who Ruled during the Golden Age of the Ottoman Empire

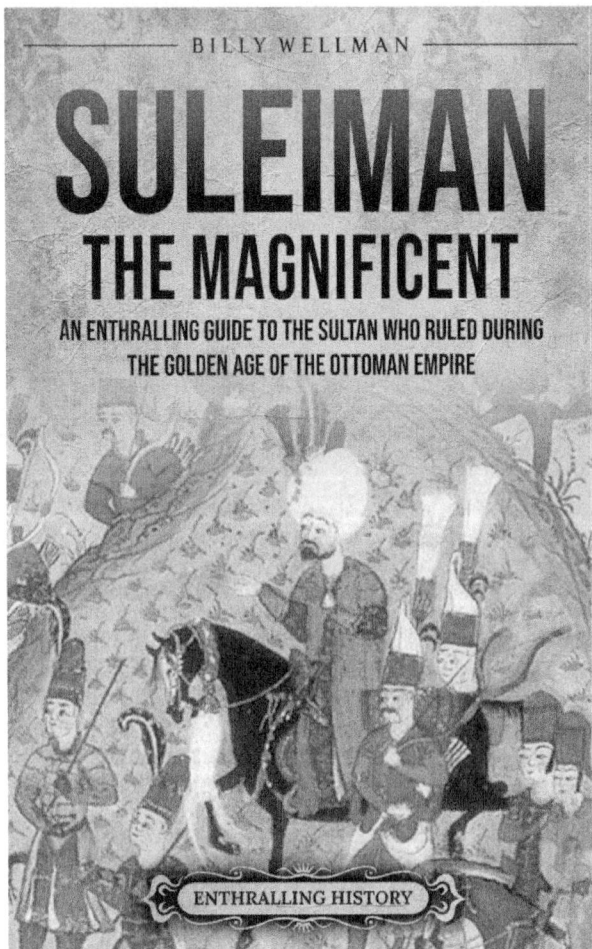

Introduction

Suleiman was one of the great figures of his age—and it was truly an age of great rulers. (Henry VIII became king of England in 1509, Francois I became king of France in 1515, and Charles V became king of Spain a year later.) Suleiman acceded to the Ottoman throne in 1520. He went on to rule for forty-six years, longer than any other sultan, and it was in many ways a golden age for the Ottoman Empire.

Suleiman's success was due equally to his political strategy and military tactics. He ensured he had good intelligence on issues, such as the balance of power in Europe, and attacked when he could see that his enemies were already destabilized or weakened. His father, Selim, had arguably conquered more territory, but Suleiman strengthened the empire's borders and confirmed its control of the eastern Mediterranean, the Red Sea, and the Arabian route to India.

However, to understand Suleiman's achievements, we must understand his background and the structure of his world. The Ottoman Empire was very different from Renaissance European societies. In some ways, it was more egalitarian since even a slave could achieve power; in other ways, it was extraordinarily brutal. Europeans have often sensationalized this history, portraying it as full of atrocities, assassinations, and harem plots. The concept of the harem as a debauched Playboy mansion rather than simply the quarters of the women and children of the sultan's family is a

Western idea. Generally, it was untrue (though apparently the "mad" Sultan Ibrahim was a sex addict and had an interesting way with fur).

Fortunately, in recent years, research into Turkish archives and historical sources of the period has helped redress this bias and show the reality of Suleiman's reign.

Even Western historians who did not sensationalize Suleiman often used only European texts as a resource. Reports from Venetian traders and ambassadors, for instance, are a key source for many historians, but it must be remembered that these Venetians would have had little or no access to the administration and none to the harem. A history of Suleiman written by Western sources is like a history of the US taken only from Communist-era Russian diplomatic sources and textbooks. The history would be partial, often based on hearsay, full of misunderstandings, and likely to have its own agenda!

This book will assume you start with no specialized knowledge of the period or of the Ottoman Empire. It will comprehensively explain the historical context in which Suleiman came to power and the culture and administration of the empire. We will cover the superb organization of his army and the discipline of his forces, both of which were major contributors to his success.

In some ways, Suleiman remains beyond our knowledge. Hűrrem, his beloved wife Roxelana's Turkish name, remained behind the screen of the harem, though we do have her letters to Suleiman and his poems to her. It is difficult to understand a man who was responsible for the execution of two of his sons and his best friend. It is difficult, too, to disentangle Suleiman the man from Suleiman the image since he is almost always portrayed in his robes of state, surrounded by opulence and magnificence. His overwhelming presence as a statesman was, of course, intended to impress foreign ambassadors, but it can make the life of Suleiman feel rather empty unless you look beyond his public image. We will try to do that.

Suleiman is fascinating. His impact on the cityscape of Istanbul was immense. His own Süleymaniye Mosque crowns the skyline, and his architect Sinan built mosques and public buildings for many of Suleiman's family and viziers. If you ever go to Istanbul, you will see just how much he changed the city, as his name seems to be on everything.

Suleiman was a poet and a goldsmith, a warrior and a lover, a legislator and a patron of the arts. And above everything else, he went his own way, jettisoning traditions when they became an encumbrance. He put the Ottoman Empire on its path for the next two hundred years and influenced the course of European history. It is impossible to understand the sixteenth century without knowing something about Suleiman the Magnificent.

This book will try to put Suleiman in his context and give you a flavor of both the man and his magnificence.

Chapter 1: Suleiman's Early Life and Ascension

Suleiman was born into a huge empire with its capital in Constantinople (Istanbul). He was the son of Şehzade (crown prince) Selim. And as far as we know, Suleiman was his only son. But he was not born in Constantinople; his father had been posted to Trabzon, on the southern coast of the Black Sea, and it was there that Hafsa Sultan, one of Selim's concubines, gave birth to Suleiman on November 6, 1494.

Suleiman was named after the biblical King Solomon, which turned out to be an appropriate name for a sultan famed for his wisdom. At the time, his father was the youngest son of Sultan Bayezid II. While there was no rule of primogeniture in the Ottoman world —that is, the first-born son did not automatically inherit the throne, as he would in Europe—Selim had two older brothers to dispute the succession with him.

When, Bayezid chose his son Ahmet as his successor in 1512, Selim was enraged. He rebelled against his father, dethroned him, and sent him into exile in a distant part of the empire. Bayezid died almost immediately after his exile, which may not have been an entire coincidence: there was speculation at the time that Selim had poisoned him. And so Selim became sultan, and the eighteen-year-old Suleiman became the successor to the throne.

The sixteenth century was a time of massive change in both the East and the West, and Suleiman was born right at the crux of this change. In 1494, the Ottomans had held Istanbul (Constantinople, the former capital of the Greek or Eastern Empire) for barely fifty years; Columbus had discovered America just two years before; Martin Luther was eleven and would, in two decades' time, split the Christian world in two. Persia was still divided among different Turkic and Mongol tribes and Arab rulers, but seven years after Suleiman was born, Shah Ismail reunited the country, founding the Safavid dynasty, which would become one of Suleiman's main antagonists. His other great opponent, Charles V (born just six years after Suleiman), would attempt to unite most of Europe under his personal rule. So, while Suleiman would inherit an empire, he would also inherit some difficult policy decisions and a set of newly-empowered enemies.

A map of the Ottoman Empire in the sixteenth century. Suleiman inherited the original kernel around the Black Sea, together with Egypt, which had been conquered by his father Selim: most of the rest of the empire was added during his reign
https://commons.princeton.edu/mg/the-ottoman-empire-1481-1683/

Suleiman would have been educated in the Enderun School of the Topkapi Palace. This would have given him the same education as most of his top administrators. He would have learned Arabic and Persian as well as Turkish; he would have studied mathematics, geography, history, law, and administration, and he would have also undergone military training. It may have been in the Enderun School that Suleiman first met the friend who would become his grand vizier, Pargali Ibrahim. Other sources suggest they may have met in a senior official's household at one of Suleiman's early postings.

Every Ottoman prince also learned a craft. For instance, Sultan Abdülhamid II was a carpenter and had a carpentry workshop in the Yildiz Palace in Istanbul, where his tools are still on display, including chisels given to him by the Japanese ambassador. Suleiman became a goldsmith—a craft he shared with his father Selim. Working on his craft would have given him time to be alone (not easy in the royal household) and allowed him to concentrate on something other than matters of state. But learning a craft was also intended to give princes humility, teaching them patience and attention to detail.

By the time Suleiman was 15, he was considered ready for his first official post. He left his father's household to become a provincial governor in Bolu and then, a couple of years later, at Kaffa (also known as Kefe or Theodosia), a major Genoese trading post before the Ottoman conquest and was still a thriving commercial center. There he would have seen the importance of the trade that was channeled from India and Persia through the Ottoman Empire and into the Mediterranean. Kaffa handled silk, cotton, and the spice trade. In a whistle-stop tour of important posts, Suleiman was then sent to Edirne and finally to Manisa.

Suleiman was also left in charge of Istanbul during Selim's rebellion against Bayezid II, a highly responsible position.

To understand exactly what was happening in 1512, the year that Selim came to the throne, a small excursion into Ottoman history and law is necessary. The Ottoman Empire had a positively Darwinian system of succession: all the male children of a ruling sultan had a theoretically equal chance of ascending the throne. They would compete against one other for position. The sultan might choose a successor, or they might fight it out among themselves. In the West, it was first born, first crowned; in the Ottoman Empire, it was the survival of the fittest.

The sons of Bayezid I, for instance, had engaged in an eleven-year civil war known as the Ottoman Interregnum after Bayezid's death in 1403. Isa, Musa, Suleiman, and Mustafa all refused to recognize the authority of their brother Mehmed. They waged war on each other—sometimes alone, sometimes ganging up with another brother. Eventually, Mehmed managed to defeat all four of them to become Sultan Mehmed I. His grandson, Mehmed II, must have heard stories of the civil war as he was growing up. He realized well how close the Ottoman Empire had come to fragmenting and sought advice from the ulema (Muslim scholars) on what should be done to keep it from happening again. The remedy was a drastic one: the law of fratricide.

Even though, in appearance, the princes were members of the privileged class, given governorships as soon as they were old enough, they were not just competitors but also playing for the highest of stakes: become sultan or be killed.

The fratricide law also prevented the creation of a hereditary aristocracy like the nobility of Europe: there were no "great houses" and no younger brothers to foment rebellion. Meanwhile, the administration was carried out by slaves and freed slaves who owed their loyalty only to the sultan himself.

Ottoman princes, at least up to Suleiman's day, were not full brothers. The Ottoman tradition was to allow each of the sultan's concubines to bear only one son. Thereafter, she would devote herself to bringing him up, training him in politics, and furthering his career. She would follow him to the sank (province) where he was appointed governor, and if he became sultan, she would become the most powerful woman in the empire. If he failed, she might find herself friendless. However, often she would find a position in a provincial court. In some cases, the valide sultan (queen mother) looked after many former concubines of her dead husband, whether as an act of charity or because they had struck up a friendship in the harem.

That was why Selim had reacted to Ahmet's nomination so dramatically: if his brother succeeded to the throne, his days were numbered. He had to fight both Ahmet and their brother Korkud to take the throne. (Following his victory, naturally, Selim had both his brothers executed. He also had Ahmet's sons and grandsons killed, apart from Ahmet's son, Murad, who fled to Persia.) Given that experience, leaving the young Suleiman in charge of the capital showed a remarkable amount of trust in Selim's young son.

Afterward, Suleiman was sent back to Manisa as governor but was recalled once more to govern the capital during Selim's campaign against Shah Ismail of Persia. He returned to Manisa again afterward. He was still in Manisa when he heard that his father had died unexpectedly on campaign. Selim was only 49. (The cause of Selim's death is still uncertain: a mistreated carbuncle, poison, plague, or cancer have all been suggested.)

As soon as Suleiman heard the news, he made haste for Istanbul, arriving two weeks after Selim's death. On September 30, 1520, he ascended the throne, still only 26 years old. Unlike Selim, he had no troublesome brothers, uncles, or nephews who might have pushed a claim. The Janissaries, professional soldiers, might be a nuisance if they were not given the customary accession gift, but Suleiman distributed gifts, gave the Janissaries a pay rise, and recognized members of the administration who had been helpful to him. Things went smoothly from then on. He was now the tenth Ottoman sultan, inheriting a united empire made by the conquests of Mehmed II and then Selim, with a disciplined army, a powerful naval fleet, an effective bureaucracy, and a fine capital city (though he would, in time, make it even finer).

A portrait of Suleiman from a Turkish manuscript.
https://commons.wikimedia.org/wiki/File:Semailname_47b_(cropped).jpg

In a 1525 letter to Sigismund I of Poland, he names himself "padişah of the White Sea [Mediterranean] and the Black Sea, of Rumelia, Anatolia, Karaman, the provinces of Dulkadır, Diyarbakır, Kurdistan, Azerbaijan, Persia, Damascus, Aleppo, Egypt, Mecca, Medina, Jerusalem, and all the lands of Arabia, of Yemen, and of the many lands conquered with overwhelming power by my noble fathers and magnificent grandfathers." This was no empty boast; he had tremendous power and a vast geographical expanse to govern.

Venetian envoy Bartolomeo Contarini saw him enter Istanbul and was impressed. "The sultan is only twenty-five years old," he said. "Tall and slender but tough, with a thin and bony face. ... He enjoys reading, is knowledgeable and shows good judgment."[1] He was wrong about the age, but the rest of his assessment is correct

---

[1] *Fisher, Alan (1993). "The Life and Family of Süleymân I." In İnalcık, Halil; Kafadar, Cemal (eds.). Süleymân The Second [i.e., the First] and His Time. Istanbul: Isis Press.*

judging by portraits of this hawk-nosed, gaunt man. (Suleiman was indeed tall judging by his kaftans, which are preserved in the Topkapi Palace. They are tailored for a man of slender build, close to six feet tall. His imperial turban would have added even more to his height. He was an imposing presence.)

Suleiman's father Selim had been noted for his severity and was given the nickname *Yavuz*, or Grim. ("Is it not permitted to put to death two-thirds of the empire's inhabitants for the good of the remaining third?" he asked his grand mufti.[2] Clearly, he expected a positive answer.) Suleiman, on the other hand, decided that even-handed justice would be the keynote of his rule.

Suleiman's first actions as sultan confirmed the way he wanted to rule. Selim had captured and deported many Egyptians, including the last ruler of independent Egypt, Caliph al-Mutawakkil. Suleiman now allowed most of the deportees to go home to Egypt. Selim had banned the silk trade with Persia; because of the prohibition, Persian merchants in Istanbul had seen their inventory confiscated. They were now compensated for their loss. The overall tone of his acts was merciful and protective.

However, governors who had abused their power were punished. Several them had allowed Selim's cruelty to excuse their own mistreatment of their subjects. For instance, Cafer Aga, who had commanded the Ottoman navy during Selim's Egyptian campaign, was accused of extortion and persecution. One of Suleiman's first actions was to dismiss him from office; he was executed in 1521.

Suleiman also drew back for the time being from Selim's dream of crushing Persia, preferring to circumscribe the Safavid dynasty's power and influence rather than attempt to eliminate it. He decided that the Qizilbash (Shia) Safavids were not, for the moment, a threat; they were fully occupied in fighting a (Sunni) Uzbek army to the east. This left him free to focus on the west for his first campaigns.

---

[2] *Clot, André. Suleiman the Magnificent. Saqi Books. 2005.*

Sunni vs Shia

Islam in Suleiman's time was divided into two major antagonistic sects: the Sunni and the Shia. To Suleiman (a Sunni Muslim), the Safavids, who were Shia, were heretics; as sultan, he was the defender of orthodoxy, so there was a strong religious element to his campaigns against the Persian Empire.

The origins of the division go back to the early days of Islam. After the death of the prophet Muhammad in 632 CE, the community was split between supporters of his companion Abu Bakr and supporters of Ali, Muhammad's son-in-law. Abu Bakr became the first caliph, and his followers became the Sunni; Ali's supporters became the Shia. Though Ali eventually succeeded as the fourth caliph (after Abu Bakr, Umar, and Uthman), he could not heal the cracks in Islam, and the split became deeper after his death.

Mu'awiya (Mu'awiyah), governor of Syria, forced Ali's eldest son Hasan to give the caliphate to him, founding the Umayyad dynasty, which was recognized by the Sunni. Ali's second son, Husayn, claimed the caliphate and rebelled against the Umayyads; he was killed in the Battle of Karbala and is regarded as a martyr by Shia Muslims.

While Shiism began as a dispute over leadership, eventually Shia theology developed in a different direction from Sunni doctrine, too. This led to further estrangement between the two sides of Islam.

Chapter 2: European Campaigns and Conquests

At the start of Suleiman's reign, the Byzantine Empire, including Asia Minor and Greece, was already in Turkish hands. The eastern Mediterranean still largely belonged to Venice, though, which held most of the islands. The Ottomans ruled Bulgaria, Albania, Bosnia, and Serbia.

Suleiman's father Selim had doubled the size of the empire, taking Egypt and, with it, the guardianship of Mecca and Medina, as well as greater Syria—what is now Syria, Jordan, Lebanon, Palestine, and Israel. He had also pushed into eastern Anatolia at the expense of the Persians.

However, Selim had made less impact on the western frontier: Croatia and Hungary still stood between the Ottoman Turks and Western Europe. And Europe had become a much more potent opponent with the election of the Habsburg Charles V as Holy Roman Emperor. Charles now wore the crown of Spain, the Two Sicilies, and Austria and, as King of Spain also, possessed the Spanish Netherlands (including most of what is now Belgium). So, instead of facing a disunited bloc of separate countries, Suleiman found himself face-to-face with a Europe mostly united under a single ruler.

Charles had also arranged for his brother Ferdinand to marry into the Hungarian royal family, with a stipulation that the throne of

Hungary would revert to Ferdinand if King Louis died without issue. Instead of being a buffer zone, Hungary would then become a firmly Habsburg property. This was unacceptable to Suleiman and made securing the Ottoman Empire's western borders a pressing need.

This was not the first time the Ottomans had decided to make a move on Hungary. In the fifteenth century, Hungary had benefited from the strong leadership of two great kings, John Hunyadi and his son Matthias Corvinus. Suleiman's great-grandfather Mehmed II had tried to invade Hungary, but Hunyadi's strong defense had deprived him of his planned conquest. Hunyadi was long dead, though, and Hungary was now weakened by the fact that Matthias had died without an heir. The great noble families saw the opportunity to give themselves more power at the expense of central government and arranged for the succession of a king they could control. They enlarged their own power and lands, stopped paying taxes, and allowed military infrastructure to fall into disrepair.

Suleiman could see how weak Hungary had become; he was just waiting for a reason to move. When the Hungarians assassinated the Ottoman envoy to Buda—reportedly sending the man's severed head back to Suleiman—he had his excuse.

The war started with great pageantry. Horsetail banners and six thousand horsemen of the imperial guard led the way out of Istanbul, and the Janissaries marched behind with their tall headdresses. Only after this show of might did the sultan appear with his personal guard. An Ottoman army on the march was an awe-inspiring sight!

Each evening, the army put up its tented camp. The inner camp, containing the tents of the sultan, the grand vizier, and the commanders, was demarcated by cloth walls from the rest of the camp. Outside this barrier, the imperial troops—those directly under Suleiman's control—were placed, and the provincial levies from other parts of the empire formed an outer circle. In the morning, they struck camp and were quickly on the march once again. Clearly, the Ottomans had not forgotten their origins in the nomadic Turkic peoples of central Asia.

But the Ottoman army was incredibly disciplined, very unlike the anarchic hordes of earlier days. The timar system, for instance, gave provincial Ottoman vassals the responsibility of furnishing a tightly-defined military force, together with its weapons, tents, and other supplies, in return for their estates. Unlike feudal vassals in the west, a timariot could be dismissed by the sultan if he did not do his job well. All land belonged to the sultan, so it could not be inherited. This prevented the rise of landed nobility, even though timariots were sometimes allowed to run in a family. It also meant that entry to the status of timariot was competitive: the son of a timariot could not take anything for granted.

Some timariots commanded entire squadrons. "Provincial forces" may not sound impressive, but the standardization of the system, together with the threat of being fired for poor performance, made them a highly effective part of the Ottoman army. Added to this were the imperial regiments, together with the border forces of the empire; all of them were professional, and all were well armored.

Next to this, the western armies were poorly motivated, poorly armed, and often unpaid. The structure of command was often unclear, particularly where forces were made up of divisions from different states.

Suleiman also had another factor in his advantage. Although part of Europe had become more unified under the Habsburgs, there were several factions that moved in the opposite direction. The Reformation was just beginning at this time, taking large parts of Germany and western Europe out of the Catholic Church. Meanwhile, Venice, perhaps the most important maritime state in the Mediterranean, was negotiating a fresh commercial deal with the Ottomans—with whom they had a long relationship—and refused to join forces with the Hungarians.

Louis II of Hungary counted on help from the West. But with Venice out of the alliance, Charles V and Ferdinand fighting in Italy, and France actively in league with the Ottomans against Charles, only the pope and Henry VIII of England helped. The pope offered money but no men, while Henry's help arrived more than six months late—long after the war had been decided. Hungary was on its own against the Ottoman Empire.

Suleiman started by attacking Belgrade, which was then held by the Hungarians. This was an important step since it would give him a forward base for attacks further into Hungarian territory. He encircled the town with his forces and used his artillery to bombard it from an island in the Danube. The Ottomans had excellent artillery capability, and artillery assault was their standard tactic for taking a town. It was not always fast, but it was usually effective.

Belgrade held its ground for two months, falling in August 1521. Less than a year after coming to the throne, Suleiman had already scored a major victory. It was all the more precious since both Murad II and Mehmed II had tried to take Belgrade previously without success. Suleiman had achieved what earlier sultans could not, and he now had a firm base from which to move further north.

The Devshirme System

The system of devshirme ("collecting") involved taking children from (mainly Christian) Balkan subjects, often from the noble classes but equally from peasant villages, to create soldiers loyal to the sultan rather than to other interests. While the earlier sultans had grand viziers who were Turks, this practice ran the risk of another Turkish family coming to rival the sultan's power and challenging his right to rule. By having the entire administration run by slave professionals, the creation of a hereditary aristocracy was avoided.

While at first sight the devshirme was a cruel system, it had its humane aspects. If a boy was the only son of a family, he would never be taken, as that would deprive the family of its heir and the parents of care in their old age. Some parents, though, actually volunteered their sons, knowing that if they did well, they could have a splendid career in the Ottoman Empire instead of remaining peasants.

The boys were forced to convert to Islam; they learned Turkish and were given formal education in military, scientific, and administrative topics, some joining the Janissaries and others various offices of state. The most talented were skimmed off and sent to the Enderun School in the Topkapi Palace, where they would learn Arabic, Persian, and Turkish and be instructed in palace etiquette, diplomacy, and administration.

By Suleiman's time, virtually the entire ruling class was from the devshirme. It was a polyglot, multicultural slave elite that was loyal only to the sultan (at least in theory, though factions did form within the bureaucracy, and some beys were known to be bitter rivals of others).

Technically the devshirme converts were slaves, but many had substantial power and were eventually manumitted. Rustem Pasha, Suleiman's grand vizier, came up through this system and was given Suleiman's daughter as a bride. His successor, Ali, was probably the son of a Dalmatian peasant; he was trained as a page, then bodyguard, food taster, general, squire, general of the Janissaries, governor of Rumelia (Ottoman Europe), vizier, and eventually grand vizier.

Having taken Belgrade, Suleiman considered his next course of action. He could have pressed on immediately toward Buda and then Vienna. However, he had an annoyance closer to home that he decided to deal with first.

The island of Rhodes, hardly more than ten miles from the coast of Turkey, had been occupied by the Knights Hospitaller after the fall of the Byzantine Empire. The Knights Hospitaller (the Order of Knights of the Hospital of Saint John of Jerusalem) was a military order founded during the Crusades—a cross between knights and monks.

The order itself was not immensely powerful, but it annoyed Suleiman by giving shelter on the island of Rhodes to pirates who would attack Ottoman ships. Muslim pilgrims who had taken ship as part of their pilgrimage to Mecca were often caught and enslaved by the pirates. Ships from Rhodes also attacked the shores of Syria and Asia Minor, threatening the trade routes between Egypt and the rest of the Ottoman Empire. The knights had also supported Janbirdi al-Ghazali, governor of Syria, in his quickly suppressed rebellion. This was not something Suleiman would tolerate; however, the difficulty was that the Knights were very well defended.

Rhodes had extensive, impressive fortifications on a strategic site at the northern tip of the island. Prominent bastions, each defended by one of the different "nations" belonging to the order, were massive enough to withstand artillery attacks and made of utterly smooth-dressed stone that afforded no chance for an enemy to climb. The Knights believed their fortifications were impregnable. Mehmed II had besieged Rhodes unsuccessfully in 1480, and that gave them further comfort. Where one sultan had already failed, surely Suleiman could not succeed?

Unfortunately, the Knights were rather weak as far as manpower. They had expected help from the rest of Europe, but as had happened with Hungary, the major European leaders had other priorities. François I of France was at war with Charles V, Venice had signed its deal with the Ottomans, under which its rule in Cyprus and Zante was unchallenged as long as it paid an annual tribute, and the pope was too poor to help.

Suleiman used overwhelming force: if Rhodes was a tough nut, he decided he would need a sledgehammer to crack it. Estimates of his navy's size vary between three hundred and seven hundred ships (as, so often, different reports give different figures). He also sent an army of 100,000 men to the coast at Marmaris, just opposite the island of Rhodes, so that they could be shipped across.

The Knights, on the other hand, had just seven thousand defenders under their commander Philippe Villiers de L'Isle-Adam. Although there were many experienced knights together with Venetian and Genoese sailors among the defenders, a large number of de L'Isle-Adam's troops were simply islanders who, afraid of the Ottomans, had sought the shelter of the fortress. So, his forces were not only smaller than Suleiman's but less experienced. The Knights also lacked the ammunition to withstand a long siege.

Given all these negative factors, it is remarkable just how long the Knights were able to hold out. Even when the Ottomans made a breach in the walls, they were quickly repelled. A general assault by the Ottomans proved a costly mistake: it lost Suleiman forty-five thousand men in a single day. The Knights' trust in their fortifications was not completely misplaced.

However, de L'Isle-Adam knew that he could not win. He was stalling for time in the hope that help would arrive from one of his allies. Suleiman offered him a truce; he refused it. But when, after six months, it became obvious that no help was forthcoming and that he was on his own against the Ottoman forces, de L'Isle-Adam sent his own terms of surrender to Suleiman. Suleiman accepted immediately. The surviving Knights were allowed to withdraw to Crete (from which, eventually, they moved their base of operations to Malta), and the Christian inhabitants of Rhodes would be exempt from taxes and from the devshirme for five years.

Although the Knights of Hospitaller lost, there was a great deal of respect for de L'Isle-Adam. He had held out longer than anyone thought he could, he had negotiated an honorable withdrawal, and he was named a Defender of the Faith by the pope. (That was a rather better decision than awarding the same title to Henry VIII, who shortly afterward took England out of the Catholic Church and pronounced himself head of the Church of England—while retaining the title Defender of the Faith.)

Once again, Suleiman had successfully conquered a fort that a previous sultan had been unable to take. However, he does not seem to have made the most of this conquest. With Rhodes as a strong base for the Ottoman navy, he could have pushed on to control the whole of the East Mediterranean. However, he had other fish to fry and left Cyprus and Crete in Venetian hands; the smaller islands, too, were left for later.

One of Suleiman's cleverest and most significant moves was not military but political: the creation of a deepening alliance with France. He had accurate reports on events and personalities in the West, and he used this knowledge to drive a wedge right down the middle of Europe. François I was Charles V's natural opponent: the linking of the Spanish Netherlands, German states, Austria, and Spain within a single dynasty was a geopolitical disaster for France, now almost entirely surrounded by its enemy.

Rather like a player in a game of Risk, Francois saw that his only chance of success was, in his turn, to surround Charles' forces—and he could do that in two ways. First, he could partner with Henry VIII of England. He tried to do that with the splendid tournament at the Field of the Cloth of Gold (named for the marvelous gold fabric of the tents that were put up to house both English and French contingents). But, despite a great deal of diplomatic cajoling, he could not convince Henry to give up England's claim to much of the west and north of France. Or, on the other side, he could flank Charles by joining up with Suleiman and giving him even more incentive to attack Hungary. Suleiman turned out to be much more interested in the proposition than Henry had been and responded positively to Francois' suggestion to make a new attack on Hungary. That would allow François to benefit from the distraction and attack

Charles' other territories.

So, Suleiman resumed his operations in Europe in 1526. The expedition followed the river valleys as far as Sofia; from there, the grand vizier, his trusted slave Ibrahim Pasha, was sent to march on the Serbian fortress of Petrovaradin while Suleiman rallied his own forces at Belgrade. From there, he followed the Danube up toward Buda (it did not become Budapest until 1873), his main objective. With Petrovaradin (strategically placed on a rock above a bend in the Danube) already secure, Suleiman knew the road to Buda was clear.

In assessing the challenge represented by this campaign, it is important to remember that in the sixteenth century, roads were poor, the weather was often more severe (more so than today), and this was a particularly wild area of Europe. At one point, the whole army had to cross the Drava River, and Suleiman's engineers managed to put up a serviceable bridge in just five days.

(Bridge building was something at which the Ottomans excelled, both in war and in peace. The famous bridge at Mostar was commissioned by Suleiman in 1557, and other bridges were built on the empire's roads. Sinan's Büyükçekmece Bridge, on the road from Edirne to Istanbul, is perhaps the masterpiece of Ottoman bridge building: its 28 arches connect three small islets to cross a shallow lake.)

But the Drava bridge was rough-and-ready, and Suleiman ordered it destroyed once his army had crossed, cutting off any easy retreat and giving his commanders no reason to argue for one if the going got tough.

The Hungarians had been waiting for assistance from Charles V and Ferdinand. However, the Habsburgs were still engaged in wars in Italy: the urgent nature of the threat appears not to have been understood by Ferdinand. This left Hungary fighting alone, under Louis II, with only eighty-five cannons against three hundred on the Ottoman side and thirty thousand soldiers against an Ottoman force of fifty thousand or more.

The Ottomans were marching north, the Hungarians south, and they met at Mohacs, an uneven plain where the hills met swampy marshland. Hungary had more reliance on its cavalry; the Ottoman army was a more modern army built around artillery and the

Janissaries, who carried muskets. While Hungarian knights were heavily armed, with full plate armor, Turkish horsemen wore lighter armor and were much more maneuverable.

Suleiman had approached on the high ground but needed to bring his army down a steep and slippery slope to engage the Hungarians. He may have miscalculated how much time this would take because his Rumelian army (one of the three major divisions of Suleiman's force) arrived on the plains before the other two wings of his army; on the other hand, he may have decided to draw the Hungarians into an attack, then flank and attack them from the sides. Suleiman's high, white turban made a highly visible target for the Hungarian army, further adding to the temptation to attack; in fact, his strategy (if it *was* a strategy) nearly misfired.

The Battle of Mohacs, shown in a history of Suleiman's reign. Suleiman, with his white turban, sits on a black horse in the middle of the picture.
https://commons.wikimedia.org/wiki/File:Battle_of_Moh%C3%A1cs,_with_Suleiman_I_in_the_middle.jpg

The Hungarians started well, with the fighting archbishop Pal Tomori leading the attack on the Rumelian army. The Ottoman army then opened its flanks, exposing Suleiman through a gap in the middle, at the head of his men and apparently very poorly defended. The Hungarians rushed in; a group of them came very close to Suleiman, killing several of his bodyguards. He was hit by several arrows, though they could not penetrate his armor.

(It is worth considering how different history would have been had Suleiman been killed at Mohacs. The Ottoman Empire might well have disintegrated; Suleiman's two sons were still infants, and both Charles V and Tahmasp I would have taken advantage of the power vacuum. Further rebellions in provinces such as Syria and Egypt might also have fractured the empire. And certainly, if Suleiman had died at Mohacs, he would not now be known as "The Magnificent.")

Fortunately, at this point, with the sultan facing imminent death, the fortunes of the battle changed dramatically. The Ottoman regulars pressed forward, and a Janissary charge with repeated musket volleys against the Hungarians, as well as heavy artillery fire, inflicted serious casualties on the Hungarian forces. The marshy terrain hampered the heavy horses ridden by the Hungarians while favoring the Janissaries and the lighter Turkish cavalry. The Hungarians were routed.

Louis II fled the battlefield at dusk, but his horse threw him into the river, and his heavy armor weighed him down. He was drowned, and his body was only found some time later. Pal Tomori was also killed in the battle. In all, nearly half the Hungarian fighters—some fourteen thousand—were killed, and a mound of two thousand heads was piled outside the sultan's tent.

Mohacs was a disaster for Hungary. It not only left the way open to Buda but also left Hungary divided since Louis had died without an heir, ending the Jagiellonian dynasty. Suleiman entered Buda without opposition, and there were rich pickings for his army. The bronze candlesticks of Buda's cathedral were taken to flank the mihrab at the *Ayasofya* (Hagia Sophia) mosque in Istanbul; they are still there.

Suleiman then gave the ancient St. Stephen's Crown of Hungary to John Zápolya of Transylvania. In return, Zápolya agreed to pay tribute to Suleiman; he may have worn a crown, but he was now a Turkish vassal—an employee who could, in theory, be fired. And his throne was not secure since Ferdinand of Austria had also put himself forward as a claimant. Zápolya was supported by the Hungarian Diet (parliament) and Suleiman, but Ferdinand had his brother Charles on his side.

As with Rhodes, Suleiman did not press the advantage he had gained with the victory of Mohacs: he looted Buda but then returned to Istanbul. Perhaps he thought his victory over the Hungarians had done enough to defend his western flank and keep the western forces divided. If so, he was wrong—Ferdinand managed to reoccupy Buda within a year.

Suleiman was forced to react. Instead of a weakened Hungarian kingdom—the *expected* result of Mohacs—it seemed he was facing a pair of aggressive dynasts, Charles and his brother Ferdinand, on his northern border. So, in 1529, he marched up the Danube again. And again, his confidant Ibrahim Pasha was appointed serasker, commander-in-chief.

Having regained control of Buda, Suleiman decided he needed to go further this time. Ferdinand was proving too dangerous to be allowed to retreat to safety: he would only return as soon as Suleiman and his army were back in Istanbul. A full-scale assault on Vienna, Ferdinand's capital, was the only way to eradicate this danger.

But the weather was against Suleiman. Heavy rain made the Danube valley a quagmire, and transporting heavy siege equipment and artillery was nearly impossible. Suleiman's supply lines became overstretched, and the rain cost him a month's progress. Though the Ottoman army was modern, it was still fighting in medieval conditions: warfare became almost impossible in winter as travel got bogged down, food ran short, and a hard freeze set in.

During that month of delay, the Viennese had taken decisive action. They had time to patch up the city walls, and the suburbs were flattened, giving the Viennese a clear field of fire in front of the ramparts and preventing the Ottomans from bringing up siege engines. All the city gates (bar one) were blocked, and—most important, perhaps—huge stocks of food were laid in.

Despite all this, Suleiman still managed to come within an inch of taking Vienna. His troops breached the wall, and he could have pressed on with an assault on the city. But the weather was getting worse, and the Janissaries were getting restless. So, the sultan decided to retreat. To keep his Janissaries happy and loyal, he gave them their customary victory payment, even though the siege had failed.

These campaigns made the Ottoman Empire a major player in European politics able to affect the balance of power. But Suleiman had come up against his match, Charles V, whose idea of a Holy Roman Empire as a universal monarchy was, in many ways, the same as Suleiman's ideology of an all-encompassing Eastern Islamic Empire.

Suleiman could not leave things there. So, in 1532, he tried again, once more with Ibrahim Pasha at the head of his troops. This time, he was not going to make the mistake of starting too late in the year and running out of time. He advanced quickly, with a massive force of 120,000 troops. If he had made straight for Vienna, he might have succeeded; instead, he turned westward into Ferdinand's territory rather than taking the more direct route up the Danube. He took several towns and castles before he arrived at Güns, the modern Kőszeg.

He may have thought that by attacking this far west he could draw out Charles V and settle the matter of Hungary once and for all. He may have also thought that taking these fortresses quickly and efficiently would give him control of his supply lines and not delay his main objective.

Kőszeg was not a significant or strategic fortress; it had a garrison of only seven hundred men under the Croatian soldier and diplomat Nikola Jurišić. Suleiman needed to take it fast and move on to make a success of an attack on Vienna.

Remarkably, Nikola Jurišić and his seven hundred men managed to hold Kőszeg for nearly a month. Again, the clock was ticking away, and Suleiman was losing his advantage day by day. During those four weeks, Vienna had been strongly reinforced, and the August rains that had helped to defeat Suleiman last time were already beginning. Kőszeg made a token surrender, and the sultan withdrew. He had run out of time and was too smart to try a winter siege again.

After 1532, Suleiman had little to do with central Europe until, in 1538, two tricky situations blew up at once in Moldavia and Hungary.

Moldavia had been an Ottoman vassal state since 1516. Petru Rareş, the voivode of Moldavia, had been received in Istanbul and given a sable kaftan (the sign of a high official), two horse tails (military banners), and the hat of a Janissary captain, but he was now suspected of joining the Habsburg cause. Suleiman had heard that Rareş had plotted against Sigismund of Poland and had been involved in the murder of one of John Zápolya's councilors.

So, in 1538, Suleiman decided to lead an army against Rareş. This time his sons Mehmed and Selim were old enough to accompany him as commanders. He took Rareş' capital Suceava, on the Black Sea coast, and deposed Rareş. (Suleiman reinstated him in 1541.) At the same time, Suleiman managed to annex much of the northwestern coast of the Black Sea, which gave him the Crimean Tatars—of whom the khan was already an Ottoman vassal—as neighbors. Nowadays, this would be called an infill acquisition, firming up the little gaps in the empire's frontiers.

The other significant event of 1538 was John Zápolya's promise in the Treaty of Nagyvárad that Ferdinand would succeed to the throne of Hungary. At the time, John was childless, and the treaty was not made public, but it sowed seeds of dissension that would sprout two years later. John married Isabella Jagiellon, a Polish princess, in 1539—he was 52, she just 20—and in 1540, she gave birth to John Sigismund Zápolya. Two weeks later, John died from a stroke.

The Hungarian nobles refused to accept Ferdinand; Isabella took refuge in Buda with the infant John Sigismund. Ferdinand invaded Hungary and was soon besieging Buda. Suleiman now set out to lift the siege, but once he and his son Bayezid reached Buda, they found Ferdinand had cut and run.

Suleiman had his chance to settle the matter of Hungary. He put the entire country under direct Ottoman rule while, as recompense, giving the child king Transylvania, which he would hold as an

Ottoman vassal. Transylvania had a much looser relationship with the Ottoman Empire than existing vassal states Wallachia and Moldavia; it paid less tribute, and no Ottoman troops were stationed there. The voivode was also elected by the Diet, not appointed by the sultan.

There, you might think, things rested—and they did, for a while. It was obvious that Charles V had neither the funds nor the military power to oppose the Ottomans. Protestantism in the west was chipping away at his Catholic Empire, with numerous German cities and states becoming Lutheran. Charles could not fight the Ottomans and the Protestants at the same time, so you could argue that Suleiman was responsible for Protestantism becoming so strong instead of being easily suppressed, like medieval heterodoxies such as the Cathars and the Lollards. Charles lost ground continuously so that, by 1555, he would have to sign the peace of Augsburg, officially acknowledging the Protestant states.

But skirmishing continued through the 1540s. In 1542, Ferdinand made another attack on Buda, again unsuccessfully. Then, in 1543, Suleiman besieged Esztergom, capturing it in just two weeks, and took Siklos and Szeged, which helped protect Buda better against future Habsburg attacks. He also captured Székesfehérvár, a particularly important city not for military strategy but for its cultural value as the original capital of Hungary and the place where kings of Hungary were traditionally crowned.

But again, Suleiman did not advance on Vienna. He was more interested in campaigning against the Safavids on the eastern frontiers of his empire. So, he agreed to a truce with Charles. But, given the Habsburgs' weaknesses, the Treaty of Adrianople (now Edirne) in 1547 was very much in Suleiman's favor. In the treaty, Charles and Ferdinand recognized Ottoman control of Hungary and agreed to pay a tribute of thirty thousand gold florins for their possessions in the north.

And so things stayed. Charles died in 1558 and Ferdinand in 1564, and for Suleiman, campaigns in central Europe were becoming a half-forgotten memory. But when Maximilian, Ferdinand's successor as Holy Roman Emperor and Archduke of Austria, decided to continue the war against the Ottomans and retake Transylvania from John Sigismund (an Ottoman vassal), the aging Suleiman had to take action.

No one knows why Suleiman decided to set out on campaign again. He had become used to deputing the business of state to his viziers and beylerbeys; he had not led an expedition personally for ten years and seems to have been in semi-retirement. Now, again, he rode to war—or rather, suffering horribly from gout, was carried on a litter. His original target had been Eger and then Vienna. But, when he reached Belgrade and met John Sigismund Zápolya, he learned that Count Nikola Zrinski, a distinguished Croatian general, had attacked the Ottomans at Siklos. He changed his immediate target: Zrinski must be dealt with first. Finally, in August 1566, Suleiman reached Szigetvár after difficult crossings of the Danube, Sava, and Drava rivers.

Nikola Zrinski set the outer suburbs of Szigetvár on fire so that he could station artillery on the ruins and retreated to the old town, which surrounded the citadel. He had a garrison of 2,300 men; Suleiman had 100,000, with 300 cannons. Suleiman set up his tent on a hill overlooking the city, but it was Grand Vizier Sokollu Mehmed Pasha who ran the military operation.

Zrinski lasted a month under siege. Having failed to take the city by general assault, Suleiman attempted to take it by bribery, offering Zrinski the Croatian kingdom (as an Ottoman vassal, of course). This was also a failure. Zrinski must have believed that Emperor Maximilian would come to his aid. He was not far away in Győr, and an attack on the Ottomans would have distracted Suleiman and evened up the numbers on each side. But Maximilian, with his eighty thousand soldiers, dithered.

Zrinski's men were dying; he had retreated from the old town to the center of the citadel. (The Ottomans were dying, too—over twenty thousand were killed by either the enemy or disease.) On September 7, things came to a head. Under Sokollu Mehmed Pasha, the Ottoman army attacked in force. Zrinski knew his time was up. He opened the castle gates, firing a huge mortar loaded with scrap iron at the attackers and killing hundreds of them. Then he led his remaining six hundred men out in a charge. He must have realized it was a suicide mission; he was killed in the skirmish. Only seven defenders escaped, though the Janissaries, admiring the courage Zrinski's men had displayed, spared many of them.

But this was not Zrinski's last stand. He had left a surprise for the Ottomans, booby-trapping the citadel by lighting a fuse that led to the powder magazine. Thousands of Ottoman soldiers were killed in the blast.

This was the seventh of September. What Zrinski did not know is that Suleiman had died on the sixth. Sokollu Mehmet Pasha kept it a close secret. He sent a message to Selim, Suleiman's successor, and forged communications from the sultan. Pasha managed to keep the pretense up for three weeks, making an orderly retreat. For a third time, Suleiman had failed to take Vienna.

Vienna remained a dream for the Ottomans. A century later, in 1563, they tried to take it once more. The Ottoman army, commanded by Grand Vizier Kara Mustafa Pasha, surrounded Vienna, cut off food supplies, and started tunneling under the walls. Kara Mustafa must have wanted to take the city intact, but this delayed things, giving the Habsburgs time to bring up relief forces and lift the siege.

It was a disaster for the Ottomans. They never got so close to Vienna again.

However, the Ottomans had won the Balkans. There are still Turkish baths in Budapest. And Suleiman was also indirectly responsible for the triumph of French patisserie: the croissant. The Viennese *kipferl*, a crescent-shaped bread roll, is said to have been made in that shape as an expression of joy at the defeat of the Ottomans, who had the crescent moon of Islam on their standard. Centuries later, the young Austrian Marie Antoinette was sent to marry Louis XVI of France. She took the kipferl with her, and the French transformed it into the buttery, flaky croissant.

This story is possibly not one hundred percent true...but it is a great story!

Chapter 3: Wars against the Safavid Empire

While Suleiman's empire had Charles V on the western side, on the east it bordered the Persian Empire. On the west, Suleiman could see himself as a *ghazi*, a holy warrior, carrying the standard of Islam into Christian realms. On the east, too, he had a religious motive for his enmity with the Safavids since, unlike the Sunni Ottomans, they were Shiites, regarded by Suleiman as heretics.

The Safavid dynasty had actually been created in Suleiman's lifetime. After invasions by Genghis Khan in the thirteenth century, then Timur in 1370, Iran was divided among many dispersed Arab, Turkic, and Mongol fiefdoms. Shah Ismail came to power with the support of Turkoman tribes in Azerbaijan and Anatolia that belonged to the militant Shia Qizilbash movement. One of his first acts was to make Twelver Shi'ism the official state religion. (Twelvers believe that only twelve imams were divinely ordained as leaders of the Muslim world and that the twelfth lives in concealment and will reappear as the messiah, or Mahdi, at the end of time.)

Once Ismail had created a coherent and stable heartland for his empire, he began to extend his territory westward. He had supported Selim I's brother Ahmed against Selim, hoping that Ahmed would give up territory to him. However, on coming to the throne, Selim retook Anatolia. This ensured that the Ottoman

Empire retained control of the major trading routes through the Levant and toward the Caucasus.

Selim had also systematically persecuted the Shia within the Ottoman Empire. Suleiman continued this, though in a less brutal fashion than his father. Suleiman must have wanted to push further east, but he knew he had to stabilize his European frontier first—he was a smart enough leader not to try to fight on two fronts at the same time.

However, the Safavids had not been given a free pass. There was another good reason for limiting their power, too. Now that Portugal had discovered the Cape of Good Hope route to India, the Ottomans' traditional control of eastern trade could only be maintained if they had full control of both the Red Sea and the Gulf routes to India.

Shah Ismail had died in 1524, and Shah Tahmasp I succeeded as a boy of just ten. Not all the Safavid provinces were convinced Tahmasp would be able to manage his inheritance: in 1528, for instance, the Safavid governor of Baghdad offered submission to Suleiman, and the Safavid governor of Azerbaijan also changed sides to join the Ottomans.

And the traffic was not one-way. In Baghdad, the now-Ottoman governor was assassinated, and the Safavids put another governor in his place. Then, the governor of Bitlis, in the southeast of Turkey, defected to the Persians. The borders were becoming very fluid, and the situation was becoming fraught.

All this started to push Persia back up the list of Suleiman's priorities. By 1533, Suleiman decided it was time to act. Central Europe was under control, and he could turn his full attention to the eastern front. He detailed Pargali Ibrahim Pasha to reoccupy Bitlis and then invade Persia, making him the serasker. The now-Ottoman governor of Azerbaijan decided to do Suleiman a small favor: he took Bitlis and sent the rebel governor's head to Ibrahim Pasha as a present. So, the campaign got off to a flying start.

Ibrahim Pasha took the Persian capital, Tabriz, without resistance. Tahmasp had run away—he was the most elusive of enemies, consistently avoiding a confrontation. He had left Tabriz just ahead of Ibrahim's entry.

But Ibrahim found the troops dispirited and tense without their sultan. He wrote to Istanbul, asking for Suleiman to come out to head the army. The sultan's presence put new heart into the troops, and they started the arduous journey to Baghdad. There, the Ottoman forces again entered the city without opposition thanks to the Persian army withdrawing rather than defending the territory.

Tahmasp's strategy was probably correct, but he had just handed Suleiman a huge advantage. Baghdad was of immense strategic importance to the Ottoman Empire because it provided access to the Persian Gulf and its shipping lanes. It was also important to Suleiman's propaganda campaign since it had been a seat of the caliphate. This helped the Ottomans present themselves as legitimate successors to the rule of the Islamic world.

Suleiman found the tomb of Abu Hanifa, founder of the Hanafi school of jurisprudence, favored by the Ottomans; it had been desecrated by the Shia Safavids. Now, it was restored, and a mosque added. In a further blow to Shia sensitivities, Suleiman took the major Shia shrines, Najaf (the tomb of the Prophet's son-in-law, Ali) and Karbala (the tomb of Ali's son, Husayn).

Holding Baghdad also gave the Ottomans a forward base. This allowed them to take Basra and, in turn, gain access to the Indian Ocean through the Shatt-al-Arab waterway. In 1536, Van and Erzerum also fell into Ottoman hands, pushing the empire eastward.

But the campaign had been incredibly costly due to the hard terrain. Suleiman was right not to push further—as Ibrahim Pasha had wanted to do—into the deserts and mountains of Iran. His logistics were already troublesome; if he had allowed his supply chain to be interrupted, the Ottoman army might have perished without Tahmasp ever having to fight. Suleiman saw the trap Tahmasp was laying for him and cleverly avoided falling into it. The campaign was finished for the time being.

In 1540, though, trouble reared its head again. Several captains had defected to the Safavids, apparently over not getting paid. Suleiman's son Mustafa was, at the time, serving his apprenticeship as governor of Manisa. (All crown princes were expected to put in time as governors of their own sank as part of their training.) Suleiman now transferred him to Amasya, further to the east and further away from Istanbul.

Some historians have represented this as a form of banishment, believing that Mustafa was already in disfavor. However, it is more likely that Suleiman wanted to protect his eastern flank while he was occupied with the Hungarian situation. The Safavids clearly received and understood the message: a strong prince with a strong army guarded the marches.

During this period, the whole Fertile Crescent had experienced an economic boom, with Mesopotamia in particular showing major improvements in its mainly agricultural economy. In Syria, Aleppo had started recovering its importance as a hub for international commerce. The eastern area of the Ottoman Empire was now proving a profitable part of the sultan's domains, and it was obviously important to protect this asset.

Tahmasp had a younger brother, Alqas Mirza, who had led the Persian army against the Ottomans. But Alqas Mirza was restless. He led a rebellion against Tahmasp, and when this failed, in 1547, he fled to Istanbul, promising his support to Suleiman should the sultan desire to invade Persia for a second time. He was welcomed with parades and numerous rich gifts. Suleiman must have felt encouraged at the prospect of a new campaign with additional support.

(In the end, though, Alqas Mirza proved a liability and fled back to his brother two years later. Tahmasp, unimpressed by Mirza's excuses, locked him up for the rest of his life—which was not long since Tahmasp had him assassinated a few years later.)

So, in 1548, Suleiman decided that, though he had weakened Tahmasp in his earlier campaign, it was time to end the Persian threat for good.

But again, Tahmasp withdrew, using scorched earth tactics to ensure his opponents found nothing worthwhile to take—no towns, no provisions, no fortresses. The Ottomans were soon bogged down in the hard winter of the Caucasus. Suleiman won some forts in Georgia, much of Azerbaijan, and the city of Tabriz (again), but in the end, he had to abandon his campaign—a second inconclusive attempt.

Tahmasp had made something of a specialty of tactical retreat, but suddenly, early in the 1550s, he decided it was time to go on the offensive. In quite a short time, he managed to conquer a large portion of what had been Ottoman territory. By this time, Suleiman tended to delegate war leadership—he was a man well past middle age, with gout that proved more and more painful—so he at first assigned Rustem Pasha as commander.

However, Rustem Pasha sent disturbing news from the battlefront. Many of the Janissaries thought Suleiman was too old to lead the empire successfully; they were calling for the now forty-year-old Mustafa to be made sultan in place of his father.

Of Suleiman's sons, Mustafa, son of Mahidevran, was the favorite to succeed his father. He had all his father's best qualities: he was brave, smart, wise, and popular with the public—particularly with the Janissaries. On the other hand, of Suleiman's sons by Hürrem, Selim was a drunk, Cihangir a humpback (though reputedly intelligent and witty), and Bayezid apparently not notable in any way.

Mustafa was not stupid. Despite numerous suggestions, he refused the temptation to rebel and asserted his loyalty to his father. So, in August 1553, Suleiman set out for the eastern front once more, greeting his sons Bayezid and Selim on his way. Mustafa was summoned to a rendezvous southeast of Konya in his turn, as he must have expected.

Confidently, Mustafa rode into the camp and entered Suleiman's tent, even though he had received an anonymous warning against the meeting.

There, Mustafa was strangled. His body was sent to the princes' cemetery at Bursa, and his only son Mehmed was ordered to be killed. This was sure to upset the Janissaries, so the plot was blamed on Rustem Pasha, who was sent into "retirement." His place as grand vizier was taken by the second vizier, Kara Ahmed. Suleiman continued the war, though again Tahmasp adopted his strategy of retreating in the hope that Suleiman would run out of steam. Selim now headed the right wing, Sokollu Mehmed Pasha the left (Rumelian army). The Ottomans ravaged Yerevan and wrested most of the western Caucasus from Tahmasp's grasp.

An exchange of insults between Tahmasp and Suleiman survives in the diplomatic archives of the Ottoman Empire. This is what diplomacy looked like at the time, with highly poetic, conventional insults bandied between the two monarchs:

"We have drawn our sword to show our anger."

"Your strength is not in the sword and spear."

"The jackal takes to the forest."[3]

But as successful as Tahmasp's continual retreat strategy had been, he could not continue it indefinitely; if he continued, he would see his entire empire destroyed bit by bit. So, in 1555, he agreed to the Peace of Amasya, which divided Armenia and Georgia between the two empires, gave back Tabriz and Azerbaijan to Persia, and left the Ottomans with both Iraq and Yerevan. Later, when the Süleymaniye Mosque was completed, Shah Tahmasp sent a gift of Persian carpets for the floor as a gesture of friendship. After more than 20 years of almost continuous enmity, the two empires had agreed to a peace that would last until after the deaths of both Suleiman and Tahmasp.

---

[3] *Clot, André. Suleiman the Magnificent. Saqi Books. 2005.*

Chapter 4: Naval Campaigns in the Indian Ocean

One of the reasons that the conquest of Baghdad and Basra was so important for Suleiman was that it guaranteed access to the shipping routes to the Horn of Africa and India. The Ottoman Empire dominated the trade routes on land from Europe into Asia, and this had become an important part of its economy. Selim's conquest of Egypt had opened up the Red Sea and the sea route to India. There had been Ottoman ships in the Indian Ocean since 1518; they voyaged to Surat, in Gujarat (northwest India), and to Thatta, in Sindh (Pakistan) and the Konkan coast (southern India).

The Ottoman navy was a key strength of Suleiman's empire—an unusual emphasis, perhaps, for the Turks, who were descended from the steppe peoples of central Asia. Unlike the army, it had not been built around devshirme recruitment. Instead, the Mediterranean corsairs (pirates), who made a good living preying on local shipping and occasionally raiding onshore, were hired to become captains and admirals. Piracy often ran in the family, just like any small business. Until this time, pirates had been useful allies for the Ottoman Empire since they could prey on Christian states' shipping while giving the sultan plausible deniability. Now, this relationship was made formal, bringing the corsairs into the empire's military force.

There was one fly in the ointment, though. While the Ottoman Empire had previously had a monopoly on the trade routes from Europe to the East, now there was a new way. The Portuguese had discovered the route via the Cape of Good Hope, sailing around Africa and up the East African coast. They also controlled Goa and Socotra and access to the Persian Gulf through their conquests of Oman and Hormuz.

The situation in India was also changing. Babur, the first of the Mughal emperors of India, had already lost two kingdoms, Samarkand and Fergana, in what is now Uzbekistan. After reconquering and losing Samarkand a third time, he had decided to set out in a new direction. From his headquarters in Kabul, he drove south, defeating Ibrahim Lodi, the Sultan of Delhi, at the battle of Panipat in 1526.

Babur had already threatened the Gujarat Sultanate of Bahadur Shah, and in 1532 Babur's son and successor, Humayun, had defeated Bahadur Shah and pushed him back to the Gujarati coast. There, he found that the other side of his realm was being threatened by the Portuguese, who had sailed up the coast from Bombay. He was forced to make a choice and decided to appeal to the Portuguese, letting them build their own enclave at Diu.

However, the relationship between Bahadur Shah and the Portuguese turned sour. Once Bahadur Shah had secured the independence of his sultanate, he thought better of the deal with the Portuguese and called on Ottoman power to free him of the Westerners. This was a great opportunity for Suleiman, opening the way to a new subcontinent. He sent Hadim Suleiman Pasha, the governor of Egypt, to assist Bahadur Shah, with a significant fleet of 80 ships carrying several hundred pieces of artillery.

Hadim Suleiman Pasha sailed from Suez and made the Indian coast in 19 days. Unfortunately, during this time things had changed very dramatically. The Portuguese had lured Bahadur Shah out to one of their ships, where he thought he could do a deal with them, and then murdered him.

The Ottomans besieged Diu together with what remained of the Gujarati army, under Khoja Zufar. The Ottoman fleet was able to blockade Diu by sea, but the Portuguese governor got a small boat out to take a message down the coast to Goa, asking for help. It also seems that Khoja Zufar, perhaps looking at the result of Bahadur Shah's alliance with the Portuguese, was becoming concerned that the Ottomans might decide to conquer Diu for themselves rather than give it back to Gujarat. Communication between the two sides became difficult, and the Gujaratis stopped assisting the Ottomans with supplies.

The siege lasted more than two months, but Diu held out. Hadim Suleiman Pasha had already decided to withdraw. If he had known that the Portuguese garrison was down to fewer than 50 men, with hardly any gunpowder left, he might have stuck it out. When a fleet of Portuguese galleys was seen approaching, he accelerated his men's departure. Bahadur Shah was dead, Diu was safely in Portuguese hands, and the Ottoman Empire had wasted its best chance to get a foothold in India.

This was not, however, a completely failed mission. On the outward journey, Hadim Suleiman Pasha had taken the port of Aden in Yemen. This gave the Ottoman Empire a foothold (albeit a precarious one) in southern Arabia. Aden was fortified by the Ottomans, and the Yemeni capital, Sana'a, was also taken. So, although the expedition to Gujarat failed in its aims, it still bolstered Ottoman power. Hadim Suleiman Pasha went back to governing Egypt (and to finding ways to spite his rival, Rustem Pasha).

In addition to keeping the route to the east clear, Suleiman expanded the Ottoman Empire in the Horn of Africa. This was probably a more opportunistic campaign, assisting Imam Ahmad ibn Ibrahim al-Ghazi in his war against Dawit II (Lebna Dengel) of Ethiopia. Al-Ghazi had taken control of the Adal Sultanate in the 1520s and—with Ottoman firearms—seized control of the Ethiopian highlands after the 1529 Battle of Shimbra Kure.

The wars continued, with Al-Ghazi pushing into the highlands of Ethiopia as far north as Tigray. Dawit II asked for help from Portugal; in 1541, Cristóvão da Gama led a small force of four hundred musketeers. By this time, Dawit had died, and his son Gelawdewos was emperor. At first, al-Ghazi and his Ottomans allies prevailed, and Cristóvão da Gama was captured in his camp at Wofla. Promised his life if he converted to Islam, he refused and was executed.

But in February 1543, the 140 survivors of da Gama's force joined Gelawdewos' army. The Portuguese contributed significant firearm resources and turned the tables on al-Ghazi in the Battle of Wayna Daga, near Lake Tana. Al-Ghazi was killed in the battle, and the Adalites were forced to retreat from Ethiopia. This was the end of the campaign as far as the Ottomans were concerned. (It was not the end of the story, though: Emir Nur ibn Mujahid succeeded his uncle al-Ghazi, married al-Ghazi's widow, and in 1559, turned the tables on Ethiopia, killing Gelawdewos in battle.)

Notwithstanding this little African excursion, the Gulf and the route to the East remained the main strategic objective for Suleiman. So, in 1548, he sent his admiral Piri Reis to Bahrain, then held by the Portuguese, to expand Ottoman power in the Persian Gulf. His objective was to seize Bahrain and Hormuz, enabling the Ottomans to block Persian access to the Gulf completely.

Aden had been lost the year before when local chieftain Ali bin Suleiman al-Tawlaki rose against the Ottomans. On the way to Bahrain, Piri Reis easily retook Aden despite the arrival of a Portuguese relief force. So, that was one objective accomplished. He then sailed onward to Oman, on the southeast tip of the Arabian Peninsula. Muscat had been in Portuguese hands since 1507, but Piri Reis captured it and plundered the city. However, he was unable to capture the fortress at Hormuz, and this failure prevented him from being able to sail onward as far as Bahrain.

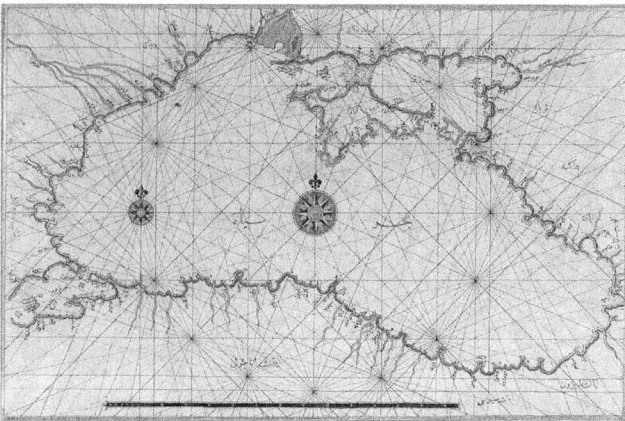

Piri Reis' map of the Black Sea.
https://commons.wikimedia.org/wiki/File:Piri_Reis._Map_of_the_Black_Sea.jpg

Piri Reis was attacked on the way home and reached Cairo with only two ships left of his original fleet of 60. Some had been sunk, while others had sought refuge from the Portuguese in the marshes of Iraq. Piri Reis had been a protégé of Pargali Ibrahim Pasha, but Pargali Ibrahim had fallen, and the grand vizier was now Rustem Pasha. There was no one left to protect him. Suleiman had him executed for his failure.

(Piri Reis may seem a minor figure in the history of Ottoman seafaring. However, as a mapmaker and writer on navigation, his influence on future Ottoman marine exploits would be immense: you will meet him again in the chapter on the artistic and scientific legacy of Suleiman.)

The Ottomans would continue to try to assert their domination of the Gulf for a while to come. In 1559, the Ottoman fleet under Mustafa Pasha set out to attack the Bahrain fort. An artillery barrage was started but failed to take the fortress. The governor managed to get a fast boat away before the Ottomans could stop it. This craft took a distress signal across the straits to Hormuz, from which a Portuguese captain sent reinforcements.

The expedition was stalemated. The Ottomans could not take the fortress, but the Portuguese could not dislodge the Ottomans. Only when both sides began to suffer a visitation of the plague did the Ottomans offer terms and sail back home. So, Suleiman never managed to monopolize the Gulf, though he successfully prevented any of his rivals from doing so.

The Ottomans did eventually become dominant in the Indian Ocean, but it seems Suleiman did not have the available resources, or perhaps the will, to assert his power so far from home. After all, the Portuguese were fundamentally traders, not aggressors—like Tahmasp and Charles V—so perhaps he felt they were not such a high priority. It was always possible to negotiate an agreement with traders. After all, the Ottomans had been doing so quite successfully with the Venetians for years.

Perhaps the biggest mystery of Suleiman's reign is why, apart from the inconclusive affair of Gujarat, he never moved on to the Indian subcontinent. Imagine what could have happened if the Ottoman Empire had added Delhi, Gujarat, Goa, and Travancore (part of modern Kerala) to its holdings: it would have been by far the greatest trading power in the East. Suleiman's military and naval capacities were far ahead of anything even the Mughals could muster at the time, and once he had secured a foothold, he would have been able to quickly conquer the smaller and weaker sultanates.

This would have deprived the world of the Taj Mahal; it would also likely have meant that the British Raj would never have existed. The world today would look very different. Then again, had Suleiman thrown all his forces into an Indian campaign, he would have risked Charles V or Tahmasp taking advantage of his distraction to stage a campaign against him. And there was a certain conservatism to Suleiman's policy: he would never risk the empire he already had in favor of one he did not yet possess.

Chapter 5: Campaigning in the Mediterranean and North Africa

Hungary was one battlefield where the Ottoman Empire came up against the growing power of the Habsburgs; the Mediterranean was another. Spain had laid claim to North Africa, aiming to make the western Mediterranean a Spanish sea, and Charles had lured the Genoese Admiral Andrea Doria away from the service of France to work for the Habsburgs. Clearly, just as much as Suleiman, Charles had an overreaching vision of how far he wanted his empire to extend. The world was not big enough for both Spain and the Ottoman Empire or for both Charles V and Suleiman.

Doria started his campaigns for Charles V in 1532 by mounting an expedition against the fortresses of Koroni and Nafpaktos in Greece, held by the Ottomans at the time. They may not have been major forts, but this action was effectively throwing down the gauntlet: Suleiman knew he had to respond or face the gradual erosion of Ottoman power in the eastern Mediterranean.

Suleiman could also see that the Ottomans needed a huge naval force to compete with Charles. In the time since Bayezid II had created the first Ottoman navy, naval technology had advanced. The ships Suleiman had were old, and there were not enough of them. Suleiman was sneaky, like his predecessors. While he set aside a huge amount of money for renewing and re-equipping the fleet, he kick-started his navy by using pirate captains and their ships as its backbone. A crucial move was the appointment of Admiral Hayreddin (Khayr-ad-Din) Barbarossa, who was made grand admiral in 1533. Barbarossa had already made a name for himself. Together with his brother Oruç, he had taken the city of Algiers, and while the two were not Ottoman vassals, they had accepted Ottoman titles. Oruç was made governor of Algiers, and Barbarossa became sea governor of the western Mediterranean.

Barbarossa quickly won back Koroni and then headed for Tunis. This city was currently ruled by the Hafsid dynasty under Muley Hasan. The Hafsids had enjoyed great wealth under Uthman in the fifteenth century thanks to being the main port for Saharan trade. Tunis also traded with Venice and Barcelona. However, Tunis' fortunes were now beginning to decline. The Hafsids had lost most of the territory around the city to various desert nomad tribes. Barbarossa must have thought Tunis was easy to pick off, and he was right.

However, he had not foreseen how Charles V would react. For Charles, Tunis in Hafsid hands was almost as safe as if it belonged to Habsburgs; the Hafsids represented no great threat to Spain. But if it was joined together with Algiers (which Barbarossa had already taken in 1516 and retaken in 1529 after the Spanish won it back), Tunis would give the Ottomans control of almost all the North African coast. That would be tantamount to letting the entire Mediterranean fall to Suleiman.

If Spain could not directly rule over North Africa, the next best thing was a disunited, fragmented assembly of different states. A unified Muslim state in North Africa was a huge threat, one that Charles took so seriously that, for once, he led the naval expedition himself. He assembled his ships at Barcelona. There were 412 vessels under Doria's command, together with an army of more than 20,000 men. Barbarossa, with his sixty galleys, quickly realized he had no chance of winning any battle and fled for Algiers.

This was the first skirmish in what would turn out to be a long war in the Mediterranean. Suleiman was already investing heavily in new and better naval capacity; he personally supervised much of the work in the dockyards. He knew that Barbarossa's decisive nature and the absence of competing commanders gave his navy the advantage of speed. The Habsburgs, cooperating with Genoa, Spain, Malta, and the Kingdom of Naples, had a more cumbersome structure of command.

The difference is easy to appreciate with a quick look at their flags. If you look up any of the battles mentioned in this chapter, you will see that the Ottoman Empire's commanders form a solid column of red standards with golden crescents. The opposing side is a mishmash of different flags—the lion of Venice, the crosses of Genoa or the order of Malta, the Papal States banner split vertically between red and yellow, the diagonal red-on-white cross of the Habsburgs, and the red and yellow stripes of the kingdom of Sicily. The command structure was, at times, as much a mishmash as the flags. Besides, Charles was always struggling financially, whereas the Ottoman Empire was wealthy and could easily afford the investment.

The other game changer was the formal alliance with Francois I that Suleiman signed in 1535. This put further pressure on the Habsburgs, and Suleiman appears to have envisaged a pincer movement to take Italy from the Habsburgs and divide it up between the Ottoman Empire and François. In 1537, Suleiman marched to Vlore in Albania, on the Adriatic coast, while sending Barbarossa to southern Italy.

Barbarossa laid waste to Otranto, at the very tip of the Italian peninsula, and was set to move further north. However, Francois, who had been expected to attack Italy from the north and move down through Lombardy toward Rome, did not hold up his end of the bargain. Instead, he attacked Picardy and Flanders, Habsburg dominions to the north of France. Deprived of support in the peninsula, the Ottoman fleet was directed to attack the island of Corfu, off the west coast of Greece, instead.

Up to this time, the Ottoman Empire had an implicit understanding with Venice: they shared the Mediterranean, traded with each other, and by a gentleman's agreement did not attack each other directly (though acts of piracy could always be used as a cover of plausible deniability). A direct attack on Corfu, which was held by the Republic of Venice, was a breach of this implicit agreement. Corfu is a relatively small island, just over two hundred square miles in area. Even today, it has a population of only 100,000. But it was a strategic holding for Venice. Had Suleiman sailed right into the Venetian lagoon, he would not have made much more impact than he did by attacking Corfu. From now on, Istanbul and Venice were at war.

Suleiman landed fifty thousand men on Corfu, attacking the Venetian fortifications with artillery and ravaging the island. But Venice had fortified the citadel strongly, on top of the existing Byzantine-era fortifications. Venice also had good artillery. The governor of Corfu bombarded the fleet and sank two Ottoman galleys; the Ottomans turned tail.

Suleiman now gave Barbarossa a mission statement. Barbarossa had a single job to do: chucking the Venetians out of the entire eastern Mediterranean.

The eastern Mediterranean is a patchwork of small islands, and most of them were in Venetian hands. Barbarossa set out to pick them off one by one, and this took him most of the year 1537— Siros, Patmos, Ios, Tinos, Astipalaia, Aegina, Paros and Antiparos, Naxos, Skiathos, Skiros, and Serifos. Nauplia (Nafplio), which Bayezid II had been unable to conquer, fell after an eighteen-month siege.

Perhaps, at first, Venice had seen Barbarossa's conquests as little more than flea bites. But it soon became evident that Barbarossa was not just being opportunistic. Venice now saw the strategic danger clearly for what it was and decided to join the Holy League together with Charles V and the pope.

Pope Paul III had come up with the idea of the Holy League as a way to bring a united Christian force to bear against the Ottomans. Charles V was quick to see the opportunity it offered him, and this seems to have led to a bandwagon effect. The pope managed to assemble forces not only from the Papal States and Spain but also from the Republics of Genoa and Venice and the Knights of Malta (formerly of Rhodes). Genoa and Venice were traditionally enemies, and Andrea Doria, who was given overall command, was Genoese—a fact that must have ruffled Venetian feelings.

Whatever the shortcomings of the command structure, Andrea Doria had over three hundred ships, including some very large, heavily-armed galleys. Barbarossa had just 122 ships in his fleet.

Doria joined the Spanish fleet near Corfu in September, and the two fleets met near Preveza at the entrance to the Gulf of Arta. Barbarossa prevented Doria from landing his forces on the coast while also managing to set up an artillery unit at Actium that could keep Doria's ships offshore. The rather fluid set of skirmishes on the coast set up the conditions for the Battle of Preveza.

Numerically, Barbarossa was at a disadvantage. But he now held the coast, and Doria was worried about being driven into Turkish artillery range by the wind. On September 27, 1538, Doria sailed under cover of darkness to the south and anchored near the island of Lefkada. He must have thought he would be safe there and could later draw the Ottoman fleet out to sea, where it would be his easy prey.

However, he had underestimated Barbarossa's bravery. At dawn, the Ottomans attacked. They had followed him south during the night and took him completely by surprise. It took Doria nearly three hours to respond.

The wind was weak, which gave an advantage to the more maneuverable Ottoman galleys and left the Venetian flagship *Galeone di Venezia* practically becalmed. Barbarossa decided to use a three-pronged strategy to make the most use of his fleet's agility and attacking power. He commanded the center, with Turgut Reis behind, Seydi Ali Reis on the left wing, and Salih Reis on the right, quickly sinking two of the enemy ships and capturing another two.

By the end of the battle, Barbarossa's fleet had taken or destroyed more than a hundred ships and had not lost a single one—though some of the Ottoman galleys had been badly damaged by cannon fire. When the wind started to blow more strongly the next morning, Andrea Doria decided it was time to set sail for Corfu, abandoning the rest of the Holy League.

There is some speculation that Andrea Doria's delay in responding to the attack and his early capitulation were due to the fact that he preferred to expose the Venetian fleet to Barbarossa's depredations. In so doing, he kept his own fleet out of danger. (It should be noted that he had a financial stake in many of the Genoese ships.)

Unsurprisingly, Venetian sensibilities had been ruffled by Doria's actions. In 1539, Venice decided to change sides; it gave up the Holy League and made peace with the Ottomans, eventually ceding its fortresses in the Peloponnese to Suleiman. This gave the sultan effective control of the eastern Mediterranean.

Preveza was a crushing defeat from which European maritime power in the Mediterranean did not recover for thirty years. And with Venice now firmly on the sultan's side, Charles V was deprived of an important ally.

That did not stop Charles from trying to oust the Ottomans. In 1541, he commanded a Spanish expedition to Algiers. However, he made a couple of strategic mistakes. First, he set out very late in the year, on September 28. Already, on his way from Mallorca to the African coast, bad weather had begun, so the fleet took three weeks to get to Algiers.

This was an amphibious attack. Charles had five hundred ships, but he also landed over twenty thousand soldiers. He decided, rather than landing on a sheltered beach a little way from the city, he would land on a more exposed shore that gave him a better point from which to attack. This was his second mistake.

The city was soon almost surrounded by Charles' troops. If he had had the time for a proper siege, Algiers probably would have fallen into his hands. But his two mistakes now wrecked the expedition. He had set out too late, and now a violent storm blew up. And he had left his ships exposed to the full force of the gale. Some of his ships broke their anchor chains and were set adrift; they then smashed into other ships. Still other ships were tossed up on shore and wrecked.

The garrison of Algiers had seen what was happening and now took advantage of the circumstances, sallying out and attacking the invaders. Charles himself was very nearly taken prisoner. A total of 160 boats were lost in the debacle, and thousands of Charles' men were either slaughtered or enslaved—so many that the price of slaves fell dramatically on the market. This was not just a failure; it was a disaster.

Suleiman was now ascendant. Further conquests came under Turgut Reis (also known as Dragut in the West), who was trained as a gunner and was a master of siege artillery; he had only lately joined the Ottoman navy and was celebrated for his accurate aim with a cannon. He had joined up with Barbarossa in 1520 and was frequently one of his main commanders—for instance, at Preveza, where he brought up the rear. After Barbarossa's death in 1546, he succeeded him as the commander of the Ottoman navy in the Mediterranean, and in 1548 he was also appointed beylerbey of Algiers.

Much of Turgut's time was spent raiding the coast of Italy and Spain or taking Spanish and Maltese galleys. But in 1551, he went for a bigger prize: Tripoli. This had been in Western hands since 1510, first under the control of the kingdom of Aragon, then under the control of the Knights Hospitaller since 1530. It was one port on the North African coast that the Ottomans did not control. Turgut Reis, together with Sinan Pasha, blockaded the fort and encircled it with artillery batteries. After six days of artillery fire, the city surrendered.

In gratitude, Suleiman made Turgut Reis the commander of Tripoli. That turned out to be a very good decision: Turgut built up the city and its infrastructure, making it an even more valuable possession for his sultan. He also used Tripoli as a base for raiding enemy ships and harassing the Italian coast. Like Barbarossa, Turgut Reis was a pirate as much as he was an admiral. Often, the point of a raid was not to extend Ottoman territory but to take captives and plunder.

The Spanish, now under Philip II, tried to retake Tripoli in 1560. Many of the rulers of the coast (Ottoman vassals, but independently minded) had not appreciated having Turgut put in charge. Several of them had been induced to join up with the Spanish. The fleet was commanded by Giovanni Andrea Doria, nephew of the great Admiral Andrea Doria.

Although the expedition made land not far from Tripoli, violent storms (together with sickness in the camp—always a danger in a world before antibiotics) made the leaders revise their plans. They instead sailed for the island of Djerba, just along the coast. They quickly fortified their camp but were surprised by the speed with which Piyale (Piali) Pasha and Turgut Reis made their way from Istanbul and Tripoli, respectively.

As was so often the case in naval battles of the time, the Western fleet was numerically superior, with 200 ships against an 80-strong Ottoman fleet. But yet again, the superior speed and maneuverability of the Ottoman fleet would be the decisive factor. It took just hours for the Ottomans to sink half the Spanish fleet. (Doria managed to escape.)

This was now the height of Ottoman power in the Mediterranean. The Battle of Djerba had crippled the Spanish fleet, which had lost experienced men and ships. And the Ottoman navy was now of considerable size and great experience. There was one major target left: the island of Malta.

Malta was where the Knights of Rhodes had made their new base. It was a tempting target for both propaganda and military reasons, and with Tunis and Djerba under Ottoman control, the shipping route to the island lay wide open. Suleiman knew that the Grand Master of the Knights Hospitaller had fewer than ten thousand men in total. On the other side of the equation, the Knights had thoroughly rebuilt the fortifications, so it would not be easy to assault the stronghold. Nevertheless, the balance seemed to be on Suleiman's side, and the sultan sent his navy out in March 1965.

With Piyale Pasha, victor of Djerba, and Turgut Reis, victor of Tripoli, both serving as officers, Suleiman had all the talent he needed. Either of the two could have commanded. Suleiman seems, unusually, to have made a mistake in putting the 70-year-old Mustafa Pasha in charge. The three men seem not to have had the best working relationship, and disagreements between them would have a negative impact on the efficiency of the campaign.

Turgut was late in arriving, and Piali Pasha advised waiting for his forces to join them before taking action. (After all, there is little point in having superior numbers if a third of your men have not turned up.) However, Mustafa decided to disembark and attempt to take the island immediately. He decided to concentrate on opening the main harbor; to do this, he first needed to take Fort Saint Elmo, which guarded it. Mustafa then started to bombard the fort.

Unfortunately, Jean Parisot de Valette, now the Grand Master of the Order of the Knights Hospitaller, had guessed that Saint Elmo would be at the center of the combat and had reinforced the garrison there. He had also given Saint Elmo half of his heavy artillery—a risk that was to pay off handsomely.

The Ottomans kept battering Fort Saint Elmo with fire from the heights of the Xiberras (Sciberras) Peninsula. However, the fort was resupplied by a ferry from the Knights' main forces on the other side of the harbor. Eventually, the Ottomans cut off ferry access, after which they managed to seize the outworks. Eventually, on the 23rd of June, they made an all-out assault and took the fort, killing almost all the defenders. But Fort Saint Elmo had done its job. It had wasted nearly four months of the attackers' time. The Ottomans had also lost the experienced Turgut Reis, who had been killed during the bombardment.

The Grand Master was now relying on Spain to send reinforcements. The defense of Fort Saint Elmo had been intended to give the Spanish fleet time to arrive. Unfortunately, when Don Garcia, Viceroy of Sicily (a Spanish territory), finally sent an advance force, it was far too small to make any difference, with just six hundred men.

Now that Fort Saint Elmo had fallen, the Ottomans could make an all-out attack on Fort Saint Michaels, which defended the citadel on the land side. They decided on an amphibious attack, which had good chances of success since the defenders would have to split their forces between the land gates and the waterfront. However, again the Grand Master had correctly anticipated Ottoman tactics, and the Ottoman boats were almost all sunk by cannons that had been placed at sea level to counter such an attack. Heavy bombardment made no impact on the fort. Worse, the Ottomans had enormous casualties in this action.

By the beginning of September, the weather was beginning to get worse, and it was at just this point that significant reinforcements from Sicily arrived: eight thousand men landed on the north end of the island on September 7th. On the 13th, the "Grande Soccorso" (Great Relief) lined up, ready for battle; the Ottomans began to retreat but were pursued, and many of them were massacred before the survivors managed to withdraw.

The expedition had been a debacle for Suleiman. He had lost at least twenty thousand men, though the fleet had come through unscathed. As for Jean de Valette, who had so well anticipated the

Ottomans' strategy and had been in the thick of the fighting at the age of seventy, he was a hero. He set out to build a new capital on the heights of the Xiberras (Sciberras) Peninsula above Fort Saint Elmo, where the Ottomans had placed their artillery. Pope Pius V and Philip II of Spain contributed to the effort, and the city was named after the Grand Master—Valletta. In 1571, it became the capital of the island of Malta.

Although Suleiman's reign saw a lot of activity in the Mediterranean and some major advances in Ottoman power, his conquests were limited by the nature of Mediterranean warfare at the time. The Ottoman navy could be a remarkably efficient fighting machine, but its forces were too often engaged in raiding or in taking individual vessels for booty, squandering a resource that could have been used much more effectively.

Actually establishing Ottoman rule was a more difficult matter. However, Suleiman's navy did manage to take the eastern islands and most of the North African coast, which changed the balance of power in the eastern Mediterranean. He also created a highly capable and well-equipped navy that his successors would use to make further conquests, taking Crete and Cyprus.

Chapter 6: Legal and Political Reforms

Suleiman was a conqueror, but that is not the way he is remembered in his own country. The Turks refer to him as *Kanuni Sultan Suleiman*, Sultan Suleiman the Lawgiver.

Sharia law, the law of Islam, was the basis of all law in the Ottoman Empire; however, it did not cover all aspects of life. For instance, specific rules of land tenure and administration were not covered by sharia law or were mentioned so vaguely that there was some disagreement over exactly how the law was to be applied. For the most part, in such areas, judges had been free to make their own interpretations of the rules. In some cases, earlier sultans had passed *fermans*, or edicts, on particular aspects of the law, and these had become part of the law of the empire; however, these pronouncements were only occasional and not systematic in any way.

Suleiman had come to the throne promising justice as the keynote of his reign. To achieve this, he realized that both the theory and the practice of law needed to be changed. For the first time, judicial power was overtly stated to be derived from the sultan, compelling the judges to follow his *kanun* or law code when interpreting the law. This was the theoretical change, and the practical change followed: the sultan was now able to codify the law and enforce his own interpretation of justice.

Suleiman therefore searched for the *fermans* and judgments made by the previous nine sultans to codify the law. He created a central library of precedents that were considered binding. Mehmed II and Bayezid II had already created law codes; he brought these up to date and incorporated them into his own *kanun*. He also eliminated duplications and contradictions.

This was a major task, but it was urgently needed; the empire had rapidly expanded and was becoming increasingly commercialized and administratively complex. Ottoman law was a sprawling mass of edicts, precedents, judgments, and advice: Suleiman simplified it drastically. Judges no longer needed to search for the texts they needed; it was all laid out for them in a structured form.

One crucial area was commercial law. The Ottoman state was highly interventionist, with regulatory controls imposed from above. The level of detail into which the law was prepared to enter was impressive. For instance, rules specified the amount of butter and sugar that had to be used in cakes or sweets and the way that Turkish baths should operate; the law also limited profit margins on certain products.

Concessions to foreign merchants, the investiture of titles to the endowment of charitable institutions such as schools, hospitals, and *imarets* (soup kitchens), and the establishment of new institutions were all part of the code. So was the law on the enslavement of war captives and on booty taken in war. In a state that was still expanding through wars to both East and West, these rules were of major importance.

Since people needed to be familiar with the *kanun* to know what their rights were, Suleiman instructed governors and judges to read it out in public. Kadis (*quadis*) were also put in charge of criminal proceedings so that corrupt governors could no longer influence trials.

Many crimes were now punished not by corporal punishment but by a fine, and these fines were laid down in the kanun. A governor could not ask anyone to pay a bigger fine than was stipulated in the law.

Suleiman's treasurer, Celâlzâde Mustafa Çelebi, also worked on the law code and was responsible for professionalizing the bureaucracy of the Ottoman state. (It was Çelebi who wrote the history of Suleiman's reign up till 1557, but he was forced out of his post by Rustem Pasha.)

Suleiman fortunately also had the full support of his chief cleric, Grand Mufti, or Shaykh-al-Islam, Ebussuud. The Ottoman Empire was in no way a theocracy; the executive and legislative authority lay in the hands of the sultan. However, the judiciary and the law courts in the Ottoman Empire were religious, run by kadis who, unlike the administrative classes, were Muslims by birth, not converts.

This was a useful way of ensuring the kind of checks and balances that are usually part of a democracy, though in a non-democratic system. A kadi could always overrule an administrator, and this acted as a constraint on both administrators and army officers. For instance, a governor who imposed what a kadi considered an extortionate amount of tax could be forced to lower the amount.

Until now, the grand mufti had been a purely religious figure; Suleiman now enhanced his status, and he became an overtly political player. Ebussuud's job was to harmonize the new administrative machinery with the existing religious laws. For instance, most of the empire's income came from agricultural taxes, so it was important that the law be robust and clear on related points. The *Kanun-i Osmani*, the "Ottoman laws," lasted three hundred years, and for the most part, they lasted because they worked.

But it would be wrong to see Suleiman as purely a secular ruler. He saw himself as a defender of Sunni orthodoxy; both as a warrior and lawgiver, he aimed at creating an Islamic state.

It had nothing in common with today's Islamic state, though. While the state religion was Islam and sharia law was observed, the Ottoman Empire respected the rights of its Jewish and Christian subjects to practice their own religions. In the case of vassal states such as Moldavia and Hungary, the government remained in the hands of the Christian nobility. The duty of the Islamic ruler was, quite simply, to bring justice: to protect his subjects from extortion by his representatives (he was always most fierce when executing justice against corrupt officials), to provide safety and security, and to create conditions in which a good Muslim could live a life of piety and prosperity. Suleiman's declaration at his ascension that he would rule with justice was, in many ways, not a political but a religious statement.

Suleiman appears to have been a man of strong personal faith. He wrote out eight copies of the Quran himself; they are still held in the Topkapi Palace museum. As the ruler of Egypt, the Ottoman sultan was also the guardian of the Holy Places, Mecca and Medina, and was responsible for much of the organization of the hajj pilgrimage as well as for the safety of pilgrims.

By taking Baghdad, Suleiman had also acquired the city of the Abbasid caliphs, the center of the golden age of Islam. The caliph was considered the leader of the entire Muslim world, but tradition demanded the caliph should be a descendant of the Prophet Muhammad's Quraysh tribe, which Suleiman was not.

This was a problem that the grand mufti found easy to solve. Ebussuud simply created a new family tree for the sultan (though he was not the first to suggest Quraysh origins for the Ottoman sultans). Now that Suleiman could see how he was descended from the Prophet Muhammed's family, he was free to claim the caliphate. His inscription on the Süleymaniye Mosque claims this, among other titles; Suleiman was the first Ottoman sultan to call himself "Inheritor of the Great Caliphate, Possessor of the Exalted Imamate, and Protector of the Sanctuary of the Two Revered Holy Cities."

Suleiman spent a good deal of money on religious and charitable foundations. For instance, in Konya, he promoted the shrine of the Sufi mystic saint Rumi; he restored the Dome of the Rock in Jerusalem and the Ka'aba in Mecca. At the same time, his wife Hürrem endowed pilgrim hostels in Mecca and Medina and a foundation in Jerusalem that still operates a soup kitchen today. The public infrastructure of the Ottoman Empire was perhaps the most all-encompassing until the creation of the modern welfare state.

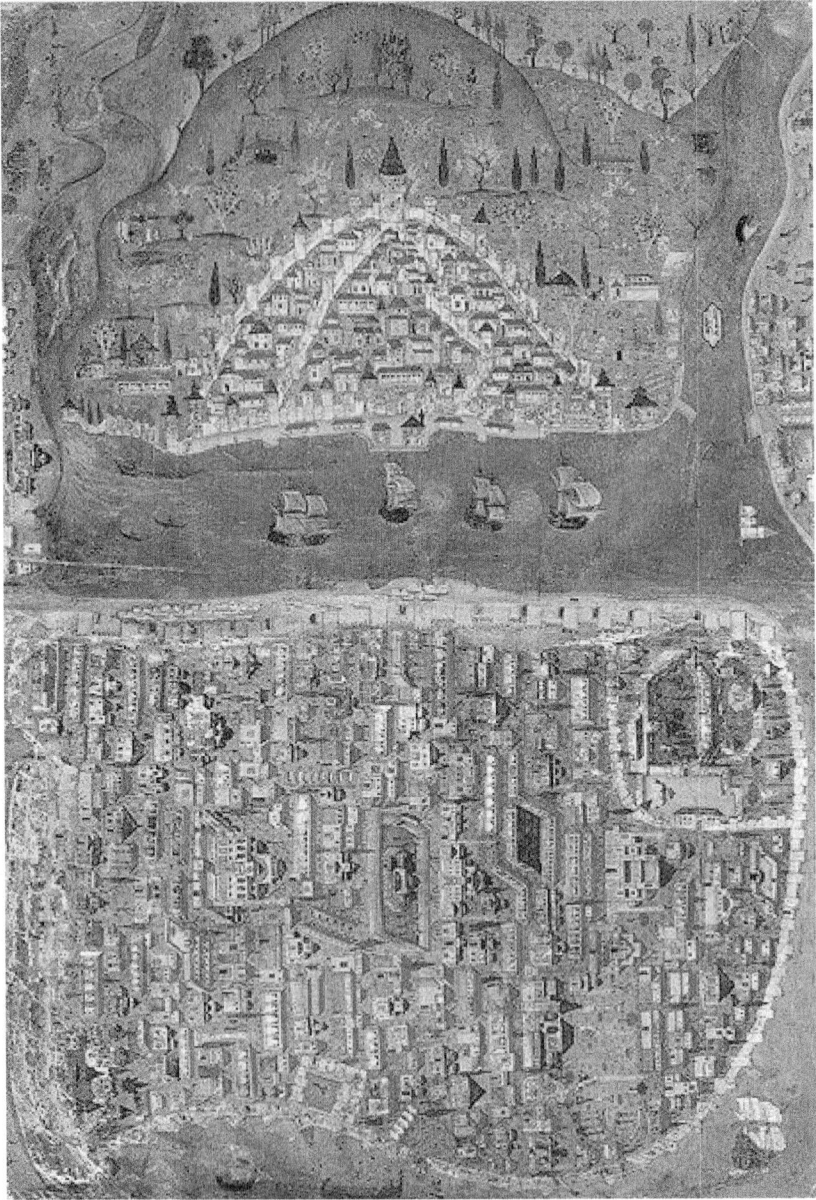

Matrakçi Nasuh's painting of Istanbul
https://commons.wikimedia.org/wiki/File:Matrak%C3%A7%C4%B1_Nasuh_-
_%C4%B0stanbul.jpg

Suleiman endowed numerous new mosques, notably his father's
Selimliye Mosque and his own, the Süleymaniye, in Istanbul. These
often included a school, which might teach up to what we would

now consider the university level. He encouraged other administrators and his family to do the same. For instance, Suleiman's daughter Mihrimah endowed two mosques in Istanbul and commemorated her husband Rustem Pasha with a charming mosque, small (not in any way competing with the sultan) but exquisitely decorated with flower-patterned tiles. Suleiman's wife Hűrrem created the Haseki Sultan Complex near the women's market, which included two schools, a public fountain, and a hospital for women.

Ebussuud, by the way, served as Suleiman's Shaykh-al-Islam for nearly thirty years. However, not all his *fetvas* (responses to legal questions) were respected. He stated that coffee was just as intoxicating and just as unlawful as alcohol. Even so, the first coffeehouse in Istanbul opened in 1555, part of Suleiman's magnificent capital. Modern Istanbul just would not be the same without coffee shops!

Chapter 7: Cultural Development under Suleiman

A sultan who was just a great warrior or a lawgiver would never be remembered as "Magnificent." But in addition to his other roles, Suleiman was a great patron of the arts and learning.

The Topkapi Palace was already an artistic hub for the empire by this time. It had been initially constructed by Mehmed II, who conquered Constantinople in 1453. He took great pains to ensure the structure would be unique; he wanted it to be unlike anything people had seen before. Suleiman renovated it during the early years of his reign to serve as a splendid statement of his power that filled visitors with awe. However, he kept Mehmed's basic outline in place.

A French traveler named Pierre Gilles wrote about the sultan while he sat on a low couch to receive ambassadors "in a little apartment built with marble, adorned with gold and silver and sparkling with diamonds and precious stones. This Room of State is encircled with a portico, which is supported by pillars of the finest marble, the capitals and pedestals of which are all gilded."[4] This was

---

[4] *Gilles, Pierre. The Antiquities of Constantinople, translated by John Ball. London 1729.*

not empty splendor, though perhaps Pierre Gilles could not appreciate the ideas and culture behind the decoration, only the expensive materials.

Like so many other things in the Ottoman Empire, the arts were highly organized. Artistic training was as much a part of palace life as administrative training, with a palace school and over forty guilds called *Ehl-i-Hirefs*, or "Communities of Craftsmen." Each guild had a pay rank structure that depended on seniority and quality of work; there were calligraphers, bookbinders, painters, goldsmiths, jewelers, weavers, boot makers, carpenters, and leather workers. Master artists would present gifts to the sultan for celebrations and were rewarded with cash or brocaded satin and velvet robes. Each provincial court of a *şehzade* (crown prince) also had its own *Ehl-i-Hiref* with the same structure.

Suleiman's was a cosmopolitan court. In the Nakkashane, the imperial painting studio, which was established by Mehmed II, there were painters from Persia, as well as from Austria, Albania, and Moldavia. This court workshop was located in the Topkapi Palace. Under Suleiman, what had been a Persian-influenced court style mixed in new motifs and influences, creating a distinctively Ottoman legacy for the first time.

Innovative design concepts included the *saz* style (of which Sahkulu was the master), which was like an enchanted forest with its twisting foliage and scattered flowers, and the naturalistic style (of which Kara Memi, a student of Sahkulu, was the greatest exponent), showing a paradise garden with hyacinths, roses, and tulips—the great Turkish favorite—under flowering trees. The saz style at its height could be mystical and highly symbolic, which must have appealed to the poet in Suleiman; *peris* (fairies), dragons, and other mythical creatures inhabit the *saz* forest, and the draftsmanship is as delicate as the subjects.

Drawing of a leaf, in saz style. The artist is unknown.
https://commons.wikimedia.org/wiki/File:Ornamental_drawing_of_a_suicidial_leaf_(TSM_K_H._2147_f._22b).jpg

A new style of documentary painting also started around this time. This partly overlaps with scientific advances in knowledge. Admiral Piri Reis' maps, for instance, are not just sea charts, important in giving the Ottoman navy accurate information about the seas it had to navigate, but a form of art with restrained color and careful shading. The artist Nasuh created topographic illustrations, including delightful images of Istanbul and even of Genoa, with Genoese ships in the harbor and triangular-sailed Turkish ships sailing across the foreground. Even the Battle of Mohacs becomes a set piece in the *Süleymannâme* (Book of Suleiman), a spectacular work; the Janissaries line up in front of Suleiman with five cannons and an array of muskets, an image of discipline and order, while on the other page the chaos of battle is shown, with a brutal horseback skirmish and Hungarian knights in their army lying dead in the foreground.

Nasuh is an interesting figure. He was not only an artist but also a mathematician, historian, cartographer, master swordsman, and navigator. He served in the Janissaries as part of the devshirme system, as he was originally from Bosnia. He wrote several books, one of which improved multiplication with the lattice system, and spoke five languages. On top of this, he was a skilled swordsman and taught students, who demonstrated their abilities during Suleiman's sons' circumcision ceremonies. Nasuh also dabbled in the arts, creating intricately detailed miniatures, some of which depict the streets of Istanbul in almost perfect detail.

The Nakkashane was a source of designs for the decorative arts, which all used the same motifs. An embroidered bookbinding, a tiled panel in a mosque, or a fine kaftan might all display the same spray of spring flowers. One favorite theme at Suleiman's court was the flower garden and joy in nature, the theme of springtime, delight, and happiness. The Rustem Pasha Mosque, for instance, is decorated with fine Iznik tiles in bold, stylized floral designs; the colors are bright cobalt blue and turquoise with accents of red, green, and yellow.

Not everything was based in Istanbul. Certain trades were the specialty of provincial capitals. Tiles and ceramics came from Iznik, textiles from Bursa, and rugs from Usak. But designs were centralized in the capital. Emanating from the Nakkashane, designs made for the court quickly spread throughout the empire. (This explains why, although not a single weaver of Persian origin is mentioned in the records of court rug-weaving, Persian designs can be found in the carpets—coming through Persian painters working in the Nakkashane.)

Some of Suleiman's magnificence was displayed in the art of spectacle. For instance, at the marriage of Ibrahim Pasha in 1524 or at the feast of the circumcision of his three oldest sons (the eldest, Mustafa, being then fifteen) in 1530, a three-week event with a mock battle between Ottomans and Mamluks, music, dance, games, and a debate between Muslim scholars. In 1536, he had swings set up in the streets, a tournament, and illuminations to celebrate his marriage to Hürrem. (The marriage itself took place in private, as befitted a member of the imperial harem).

This magnificence was only temporary, like that of the Field of the Cloth of Gold in which Henry VIII and François I tried to outdo each other with the quality of their accouterments, or the coronation of Charles V as emperor at Bologna, at which fountains poured red and white wine. (Ottoman sultans' accessions, unlike coronations, were entirely practical affairs.) More permanent remains of such spectacle are the many ceramic and metal vessels and lamps in the Topkapi Palace and elsewhere, as well as ornate display armor that belonged to Suleiman and his household.

In particular, an amazing treasury of wonderful textiles survives thanks to the tradition of placing a coffer of clothes in the mausoleums of the sultan's family. Suleiman's personal clothing was often made of the palest shades. His clothing was elegant and refined but austere; his sons' kaftans, on the other hand, were made in bright floral and geometrically patterned fabrics with a palette of bright red, pistachio green, yellow, and blue, sometimes on an almost black background or with highlights woven with silver and gold thread.

Suleiman's greatest single bequest to posterity, though, is the architecture of his reign. He started by adding a hospital and *hammam* (Turkish bath) to his mother's charitable foundation at Manisa in 1538; at the same time, Hürrem was creating her first foundation in Istanbul, architecturally unassuming (perhaps determined not to compete with Suleiman's work) but with a magnificent level of public services provided. Suleiman's sister, Sah Sultan, endowed three mosques, three dervish houses, and other smaller projects.

Truly great people often distinguish themselves by the support they provide for others to perform at the highest level. Suleiman will forever be remembered as the patron of the architect Sinan. And if the first half of his reign can be seen as the time of Ottoman expansion, the second half became that of construction.

Sinan was not just an architect but an engineer. Originally Armenian or Greek, he had been conscripted—he fought at Mohacs—and knew how to destroy buildings efficiently by artillery fire and build bridges and fortifications. His first imperial commission was Hürrem's Haseki Sultan Complex. Mihrimah Sultan then gave him the commission for her Iskele Mosque on the waterside in Uskudar, opposite Istanbul.

When Suleiman's son Mehmed died at just twenty-two years of age, the sultan ordered Sinan to build a mosque in his memory, the Şehzade (crown prince) Mosque. Once that was completed, in 1550, Suleiman commissioned his own mosque, the Süleymaniye, high above the Golden Horn. These and the Selimliye Mosque in Edirne that Sinan built for Suleiman's successor, Selim II, are his masterpieces. At the same time, he was working on numerous bridges, caravanserais, *hans*, and even aqueducts, as well as on smaller commissions like the Rustem Pasha Mosque.

Mosques were not just places of worship. They were almost always part of complexes that might include theology and law schools, mausoleums, public kitchens known as *imarets*, hospitals, inns, and other useful services. Some mosques were built above a high basement that included shops; the shops paid rent to the mosque, which paid its maintenance expenses. The Süleymaniye Mosque included at least four colleges, a soup kitchen, caravanserai, a hospital, an asylum, a *tabhane* (a travelers' hospice), and a *hammam*.

The interior of the Süleymaniye Mosque, Istanbul.

None of what Sinan did was original. All the individual elements, such as the high vaulted basement, slender minarets, central flattish dome, and broad double portico in front, had already been used in Ottoman architecture. What *was* original was the way Sinan took existing elements and formats and combined them into what became the classical style of the Ottoman Empire. So far, buildings had been created in an accretive way, by adding separate pieces together, but Sinan—perhaps inspired by the great Byzantine church of Hagia Sophia—created buildings that were coherent, both outside and inside. In particular, he aimed to produce an undivided, cohesive interior space.

Suleiman's Istanbul was a center of the sciences and the arts. Piri Reis, one of his most experienced admirals, was known as a cartographer. His *Kitab-i Bahriye* (Book of Navigation) contains detailed sea charts of the Mediterranean, and his world map is the earliest Turkish atlas to show the New World. Seydi Ali Reis contributed the *Mirat-ul Memalik* (Mirror of Countries) and navigational textbooks.

You might recall Seydi Ali Reis from before; he was one of the commanders during the Battle of Preveza in 1538. He would become an admiral of the Ottoman fleet in the Indian Ocean and fought the Portuguese, who had interests in the region. His books are some of the most important works from this time period, as they cover ways to calculate time, how to use the stars properly as a guide, wind and sea currents, important ports and harbors, and how to use a compass, among other things.

Art overlapped with law, too: for instance, in the beautiful tughra, or calligraphic signature, which was attached to every *ferman* sent out by the sultan. A tughra can be simple, as drawn by a lawyer, or beautiful, as drawn on an important document by a professional calligrapher, the spaces filled with flowers and leaves and illuminated in gold.

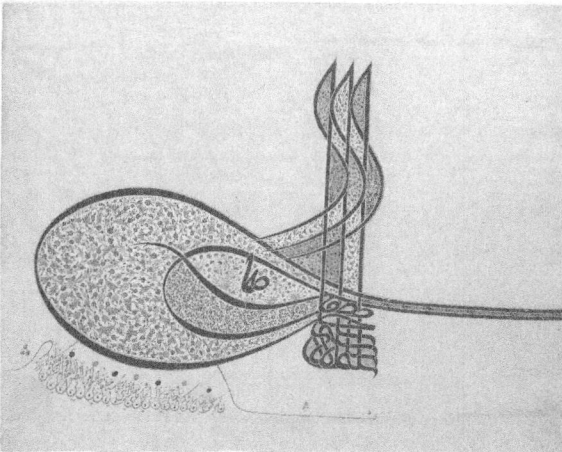

Tughra of Sultan Suleiman, in the Metropolitan Museum, New York.
https://www.metmuseum.org/art/collection/search/449533

And, of course, there was literature. Suleiman himself was both a goldsmith by trade and a poet by disposition. It is easy to write off rulers as being subpar poets since they had bigger things on their plate to deal with than focusing on flowery language, but most historians agree that he was a great poet. He wrote under the pen name of Muhibbi (Lover), in both Persian and Turkish, and one of his verses is still often quoted: "Men think of wealth and power as the greatest fate; but in this world, a spell of health is the best state. What men call sovereignty is worldly strife and constant war; Worship of God is the highest throne, the happiest of estates."[5]

---

[5] *Halman, S. Talat. Poems by Suleyman the Magnificent under the pseudonym Muhibbi. Millenium. 2007.*

Chapter 8: Suleiman's Family Life

Ottoman sultans had no real family life—a stark statement but very true for most sultans. They were the slaves of their fate and the servants of their dynasty. The laws of the harem compelled them to give up a concubine as soon as she bore a son. Their brothers and sons, uncles and nephews, were all rivals for the throne in the ultra-competitive, almost Darwinist system of rule. Though Mehmed III was exceptional in the scale of his fratricide when he murdered 19 of his brothers upon his accession, many sultans had killed brothers or sons who rebelled against them or were thought likely to rebel. Only mothers and their daughters could be loved unconditionally and without fear of them either becoming rivals or having to be sent away. The harem was not a place of pleasure but a living unit with iron laws.

Until Suleiman's reign, sultans did not even live in the same palace as their concubines and children. They occupied the Old Palace, at the other end of the long Divan Yolu street, while the sultan lived in the "new" Topkapi Palace. The whole structure was arranged to ensure that separate centers of power could not be set up and that there was proper competition between the sultans' sons, ensuring the survival of the fittest—and, of course, the death of the others. Suleiman, however, stepped outside these boundaries and created a nuclear family.

The one major relationship in a sultan's life was that with his mother. A prince's mother would accompany him on his first tour of duty in the provinces and would oversee the domestic arrangements of his court, including managing the harem. As a young man, Suleiman was no exception to this rule. His mother Hafsa accompanied him on his first political assignment as the governor of Caffa (Kefe), on the shores of the Crimean Peninsula. She was most likely a captive and a slave (though some sources call her a Tatar princess) and would have gone through the same process of acclimatization and education as Suleiman's concubines. (Caffa, ironically, was a center of the Tatar slave trade; Hafsa may well have seen it once before if she had passed through on her way to Istanbul's slave markets.)

The first of Suleiman's concubines that we know of was Mahidevran, the mother of Şehzade Mustafa. She had already given birth to Mustafa while Suleiman was in Manisa. The second (and last) of his concubines was Hürrem Sultan, who became the love of Suleiman's life. After Hürrem, he appears to have had no other concubines.

Hürrem is known in the West as Roxelana. This is said to be because she had red hair, but it is more likely because she was a "Russian." She may well have come from Ukraine and certainly came from a Christian family. The Ottoman sultans took their concubines only from Christian families, enslaved and converted to Islam. This, like the law of fratricide and the devshirme system, reflected the Ottoman suspicion of any potential rival to the dynasty. Concubines, unlike western queens, had no family ties that might run counter to the Ottoman dynasty's interests. "Roxelana," whatever her original name, was soon renamed Hürrem, which means "joyful."

Female slaves were trained in the Old Palace to create an elite class of female slaves; they would have learned needlework, Turkish, etiquette, music, dance, and sometimes calligraphy. They would learn to read and write, perhaps not perfectly. Smart girls would have picked up a good sense of how to play the politics of the harem, too—and Hürrem was certainly smart.

There is a story that she was given to Suleiman as a gift, either by his mother Hafsa or by Pargali Ibrahim, his male favorite. Suleiman already had four children when he came to the throne. In accordance with tradition, they all had separate mothers. There was Mahmud, Mustafa, Murad, and a daughter, Raziye Sultan. But only Mustafa, son of Mahidevran, survived an epidemic in 1521 which killed all the others. (This was a dreadful family tragedy and spoiled what should have been a joyful time for Suleiman. His first son with Hürrem, Mehmed, the first son of a sultan to be born in Istanbul in nearly half a century, had just been born; he had captured Belgrade, a major cause for celebration. Yet the first news he received on his return to Istanbul was that of the death of three of his children.)

Hürrem bore their first child within a year of Suleiman's accession, and by 1534, they had five children: Mehmed, Mihrimah, Selim, Bayezid, and crippled Cihangir. (Abdullah, a sixth, had died of smallpox in 1528.) Meanwhile, Suleiman's mother Hafsa had died, leaving Hürrem at the head of the harem. Suleiman had already broken with the convention that a concubine could only bear the sultan one son; he and Hürrem had four living sons and were effectively a monogamous couple. In 1534, he broke convention even more definitively by freeing Hürrem and then marrying his freed slave. The marriage celebration was spectacular, with a procession of giraffes and other wild animals, a great tournament, music, and feasts. This was all reported by the Western ambassadors, though none of them seem to have realized just how out of the ordinary this celebration was.

Out of the imperial harem, Hürrem created an institution of power rather than simply a residence for the sultan's concubines. Due to her example, later royal women had real influence as wives and as valide sultan (mother of the sultan)—at times, even as regents. She was the first royal wife to live in the Topkapi Palace, not in the Old Palace. This marks an "important shift in the gender demographics of power," according to historian Leslie Peirce.[6] Hürrem's mosque at Manisa was the first built by a prince's mother to have two minarets. Until then, this had been a prerogative of the sultan alone.

---

[6] Peirce, Leslie. Imperial Harem: *Women and Sovereignty in the Ottoman Empire*. Oxford University Press. 1993.

A portrait of Hűrrem by a Venetian artist. It is worth pointing out that no Venetian would ever have seen inside the harem, so this "portrait" is probably a work of pure imagination.
https://commons.wikimedia.org/wiki/File:Portrait_of_Roxelana_(aka_Hurrem_Sultan).jpg

Hűrrem was politically active enough to write letters to queens in Europe. She wrote to John Zápolya's mother, Isabella, and to Isabella's mother, Bona Sforza, queen of Sigismund the Old of Poland. Mihrimah followed her mother's example of holding an extensive diplomatic correspondence.

Hűrrem also appears to have started the tradition of female philanthropy in the capital, founding mosques, hospitals, schools, soup kitchens, Sufi lodges, caravanserai, and shrines. Her daughter Mihrimah continued this tradition of open-handedness, creating several mosques and completing her husband Rustem Pasha Mosque after his death. A form of trickle-down economics seems to have operated. For example, Hűrrem's slave woman Nevbahar used building materials left over from the building of Hűrrem's

Haseki Sultan Mosque to renovate a nearby mosque, which was then named after Nevbahar.

It is true that Bayezid's concubines had already endowed charitable foundations and that Suleiman's mother Hafsa had created a new foundation in Manisa. But, until Hűrrem, no royal concubine had ever built anything in Istanbul itself. To build in the capital was a statement of some importance.

Suleiman enjoyed years of happiness with his young family, but tragedy struck his life again when the eldest of his sons with Hűrrem, Şehzade Mehmed, died at age 22. Again, it was news that ruined a homecoming, as Suleiman only found out that his son had died when returning to Istanbul from a Balkan campaign. And again, Suleiman decided that his feelings were a strong enough reason to break with precedent. Princes were almost always buried in Bursa, the former Ottoman capital. Suleiman decided that, instead, Mehmed would find his resting place in Istanbul. The Şehzade Mosque, which commemorates his son, was his first commission from Sinan.

Suleiman's grief over Mehmed's death was legendary. He wept for over two hours and kept forty days of mourning, continually dressed in black. As a father, sultan, and poet, he gave Mehmed a last tribute: "My Sultan Mehmed, distinguished among princes."[7] (It is cleverer than it looks. The little verse is a chronogram in which the numerical value of the letters adds up to the year of his son's death. The intricacy of this conceit reflects the goldsmith just as much as the poet.)

Suleiman's other sons, in accordance with Ottoman custom, were sent to rule provincial cities as soon as they were old enough. Mustafa was sent to Amasya with his mother Mahidevran; Selim, sent to Konya, did not have the advantage of his mother Hűrrem with him since she stayed in Istanbul with Suleiman. Yet again, this marked an abandonment of tradition since accompanying a son to his provincial posting had always been the career pattern for

---

[7] Peirce, Leslie. Imperial Harem: *Women and Sovereignty in the Ottoman Empire*. Oxford University Press. 1993.

concubine mothers.

Suleiman appears to have adored his daughter, Mihrimah Sultan, and she was an important figure in his court. She was married to Grand Vizier Rustem Pasha, apparently not entirely in accordance with her wishes. However, when she told her father that Rustem Pasha was a leper, he called her bluff by having the vizier examined by doctors; since they found their patient was perfectly healthy, Mihrimah had to agree to the marriage.

In fact, marriage to a high-ranking civil servant had become traditional for daughters of the sultan—one tradition that Suleiman did not break. After Rustem Pasha's death, she volunteered to marry the new vizier, Semiz Ali Pasha, but he appears to have declined the offer, and she remained unmarried thereafter.

When Hürrem died in 1558, Mihrimah became her father's confidant. Father-son relations in the Ottoman Empire were always fraught; a daughter, on the other hand, could offer unqualified support to her elderly father. When her brother Selim succeeded to the throne, she lent him money and apparently gave him advice; she lived to see her nephew Murad III become sultan in 1574. She sponsored two mosques built by Sinan: the Iskele Mosque in Üsküdar in 1543 and the Mihrimah Sultan Mosque, beside the Edirne Gate, in 1562. She is the only one of Suleiman's children to be buried beside him in his mausoleum at the Süleymaniye Mosque.

Suleiman's final years were difficult. He had started suffering from gout sometime during his middle years, one reason he spent more time in Istanbul and less on campaign. His sons were all nervously considering their chances of succession. He now had four surviving sons: Mustafa (who was popular with the army), Selim, Bayezid, and Cihangir. Of the four, only Cihangir could be ruled out as sultan due to his handicap. Mustafa was already building support for an eventual bid for the throne after his father's death, as he knew he would have to fight his half-brothers. Lining up that support was normal under the circumstances and did not mean Mustafa intended to cut his father's reign short.

But Suleiman must have worried that one of his sons would jump the gun. Perhaps he was remembering how his father Selim had dethroned Bayezid II. So, when he heard the rumors of

Mustafa being proposed by the Janissaries as the next sultan, he may have rushed to judgment without due consideration. Alternatively, he may have decided that if the army was tiring of his rule and actively supporting Mustafa, it was just too dangerous to leave Mustafa alive.

The Janissaries were not yet all-powerful, though Suleiman respected their power enough to have given them bonuses and raises on his accession. Later, they became powerful enough to impose their own choice of sultan. In 1622, the Janissaries deposed Osman II, who was strangled the next day and replaced by his uncle, the previously deposed sultan, Mustafa I.

However, many contemporaries believed that Mustafa's execution was not Suleiman's idea and that he initially opposed it. Hürrem and Mihrimah, rumors said, had worked with Rustem Pasha to ensure Şehzade Mustafa's downfall. Hürrem was motivated by the desire to cut Mahidevran's son out of the succession and, in particular, ensure that Bayezid (apparently his mother's favorite) would succeed to the throne.

Mustafa was said to have received foreign ambassadors and Ottoman commanders without Suleiman's knowledge, which would have justified his execution if true. However, Mustafa was widely held to be innocent, and Rustem Pasha took the blame. Rustem had reported the rumors to his sultan, so he might have been acting as an agent provocateur on behalf of Hürrem Sultan. He might even have framed Mustafa by inventing evidence. On the other hand, he may have just been looking after Suleiman's interests.

The fact that Rustem was reinstated after a temporary exile certainly points to the idea that he was being used as a scapegoat. Suleiman needed someone to take the blame. All sultans did. Being all-powerful was a problem since you took the blame for everything unless you handed it on to someone else. That was why so many grand viziers were executed; there was no better way to shift the blame. Rustem Pasha was lucky to receive exile rather than death as his punishment.

However, the fact that he was made a scapegoat does not mean, necessarily, that he was working for Hürrem.

Cihangir died shortly after Mustafa's execution. Some people said he died of grief for the dead Mustafa; it seems more likely that he died because of his disabilities. A fake Mustafa appeared in Rumelia and caused a certain amount of worry, but he was captured, brought to Istanbul, and executed. Bayezid was suspected of involvement, or at least of having been very slow to take action against the pretender, but Hűrrem protected her favorite son. After her death in 1558, though, no one was left to protect him, and the aging Suleiman was now anxious about potential rebellions.

Bayezid had managed to attract many of Mustafa's supporters. Suleiman now suspected that Bayezid might ask for support from the Persians; he therefore put all his forces under his son Selim and sent him to war against Bayezid. Selim defeated Bayezid at Konya in 1559; Bayezid escaped and fled to Persia with his four sons (maybe putting some meat on the bones of the idea he had been seeking Persian support). He was greeted with a magnificent display of hospitality by Tahmasp.

It would not last. Suleiman asked Tahmasp to execute Bayezid or hand him over to the Ottomans, but Tahmasp refused: it would not be honorable to execute someone to whom he had shown hospitality. However, Suleiman continued to negotiate, and eventually, it appears the suggestion that Tahmasp might, given the right consideration, simply turn a blind eye was persuasive. A Turkish executioner was sent to Persia, and Bayezid was strangled, together with all his surviving sons; one of them, Şehzade Mehmed, was only three years old.

This left Şehzade Selim as Suleiman's sole successor, just as Suleiman had been sole successor to Selim I.

Suleiman had probably killed the best of his sons, leaving the empire in the hands of a mediocre drunk. But at least he had avoided a fratricidal war after his death and handed the empire to Selim unencumbered and entire. His feelings on these deaths are unrecorded; perhaps after Mehmed's death, he had no love left for his other sons.

Chapter 9: Suleiman and Grand Vizier Ibrahim Pasha

A slave could rise through the devshirme system and education in the Topkapi Palace School to the highest office of state. And any grand vizier could fall from that height. Ibrahim Pasha was a prime example of the Ottoman wheel of fortune: a sudden rise and a fall equally as sudden.

The devshirme system made it easy for a sultan to appoint the viziers of his choice—and just as easy to depose them since viziers had no extended family to be offended. In Europe, the major noble houses often represented a challenge for the monarch to manage. Dynastic struggles such as the Wars of the Roses in England show how easily a king could lose control: sacking a Lord Chancellor could lead to a rebellion. This simply was not the case in the Ottoman Empire.

Pargali Ibrahim was likely Greek or Albanian. As with many of the devshirme pashas, we do not know his ethnic origin or his name before his conversion to Islam. Born in 1493 in Parga, a village on the coast of the Adriatic Sea, he was given his nickname Pargali after his birthplace.

Pargali might have met Suleiman at the palace school, but some sources indicate he was bought as a slave by Iskender Pasha, the governor of Bosnia, and first met Suleiman at Iskender Pasha's estate near Edirne. He was thin, pale, and graceful, but not a tall man like Suleiman; he played the violin and could speak Italian and Persian as well as Turkish. One of the qualities Ibrahim shared with Suleiman was a lively mind. He was an inquisitive man who sought out all kinds of knowledge and was reported to have said that a man who does not try to learn everything he can is incompetent.

Suleiman soon took him into his household, and there are suggestions he may also have taken him into his bed. Whether or not they were lovers, the bond between the two men was remarkably close. Suleiman made Ibrahim his chief falconer. When he acceded to the throne, he promoted Ibrahim to *Khass-Oda-Bashi*, the head of the sultan's chamber. This was a position of great influence since he was always in contact with the emperor, awake or asleep, and held one of the seals of the empire.

Suleiman inherited Selim's grand vizier, Piri Mehmed Pasha, but kept him only a few years before replacing him in 1523 with Ibrahim, using Piri Mehmed's age (he was nearing sixty) as a rationale. Ibrahim's appointment as grand vizier straight from head page of the privy chamber was unprecedented. Normally, viziers worked their way up systematically through the ranks. No doubt his promotion made him enemies with some of the other bureaucrats.

In 1524, Ibrahim's marriage was celebrated on the maidan, the former Greek hippodrome, with huge celebrations over two weeks. Marriage marked adulthood and, for the devshirme, integration into the political elite. Earlier histories say that Ibrahim married Suleiman's sister, Hatice Sultan. However, recent research suggests that he actually married the granddaughter of Iskender Pasha, Muhsine Hatun. In another breach with tradition, Ibrahim kept his bedroom next to the sultan's, in the inner court of the palace, even after he had married.

Suleiman always delegated a great deal of power to his viziers, preferring to rule from the seclusion of the palace when he was not leading his troops. This was partly intended to create a feeling of awe at the invisible sultan, making his forays out of the palace all the rarer and more spectacular, but Suleiman also appears to have valued his privacy. The grand vizier was expected to take a great deal of the burden of running the state, which by now was a much larger and more complex empire than in the time of the earlier Ottoman sultans.

While he was grand vizier, Ibrahim Pasha was also beylerbey of Rumelia, with responsibility for all Turkey's European possessions. The revenues from this position, added to his emoluments as vizier, made him one of the richest men in the empire, and he loved to flaunt his wealth. Venetian diplomats noted that he often appeared much more richly dressed than the sultan and wearing more jewelry. His palace on the maidan was huge and sumptuous; it is now the Museum of Turkish and Islamic Arts.

At the time, Ibrahim was referred to as "Il Magnifico" and Suleiman only as "Il Signor" (the Lord). He accepted and even solicited presents from courtiers and foreign diplomats but, with rigid honesty, refused to take bribes.

Egypt, which had been conquered by Suleiman's father Selim, was still not completely subdued, and in 1524, the Ottoman governor of Egypt, Hain Ahmed Pasha, decided to declare his independence. His rule did not last long; he fled Cairo, but the Ottoman authorities caught and executed him. Suleiman now decided to give Ibrahim the job of reforming the entire system of government, both civil and military.

It was a tricky situation because, in taking Egypt from the Mamluk Sultanate, the Ottoman Empire had taken over a country that was Arab, not Turkish, and therefore had very different customs from the Ottomans. Ibrahim was clever and astute. He created a system in which the subsidiary beys acted as a check on the powers of the beylerbey so that the governor could no longer control the entire machinery of state. This greatly reduced the chances of future rebellion.

It was also an incredibly important thing to get right. Egypt was commercially and economically crucial to the Ottoman Empire; it made a massive tax contribution and opened the way to the Red Sea, India, and points further east. The Ottomans even started a canal from the Red Sea to the Nile, a predecessor of the Suez Canal that was intended to provide an alternative route for the spice trade.

Suleiman evidently had huge confidence in Ibrahim, and Ibrahim rewarded it.

Ibrahim's next major project was as commander of the imperial army at Mohacs. He claimed responsibility for the victory. That makes him look a bit of a braggart, but in fact, Suleiman, in a letter of victory, also proclaims the victory as Ibrahim's, calling his Pasha "the leopard of strength and valor, the tiger of the forest."[8] There was always a great deal of poetry and compliment in official communications; the truth is probably that both men molded the strategy and helped carry it out as partners rather than monarch and inferior.

Ibrahim was not always at war with the West; he was often used as Suleiman's go-between for negotiating tactically with Christian powers. His linguistic skills were helpful in allowing him to speak to Italian ambassadors and merchants directly while in Istanbul, so no doubt he was better informed than many members of the administration on Western matters. He was close to the Venetians Pietro Zen and Alvise Gritti (the illegitimate son of a Doge of Venice), which would also have given him a good understanding of Western customs and politics. In 1533, he secured Charles V's agreement to make Hungary an Ottoman vassal state, and in 1535, he helped negotiate the agreement with Francois I, giving the French preferential trading rights in return for joint action against the Habsburgs.

Ibrahim was glamorous, but he made his sultan glamorous, too. Having seen what Western crowns were like, he asked Alvise Gritti to help him create a European-style crown for the sultan. Engravings of Suleiman wearing it were long thought to be fakes, the artists' invention, but records show it did exist. Suleiman did not wear it but frequently displayed it to impress ambassadors and other visitors.

---

[8] Jenkins, Hester Donaldson. Ibrahim Pasha: Grand Vizier of Suleiman the Magnificent (1911).

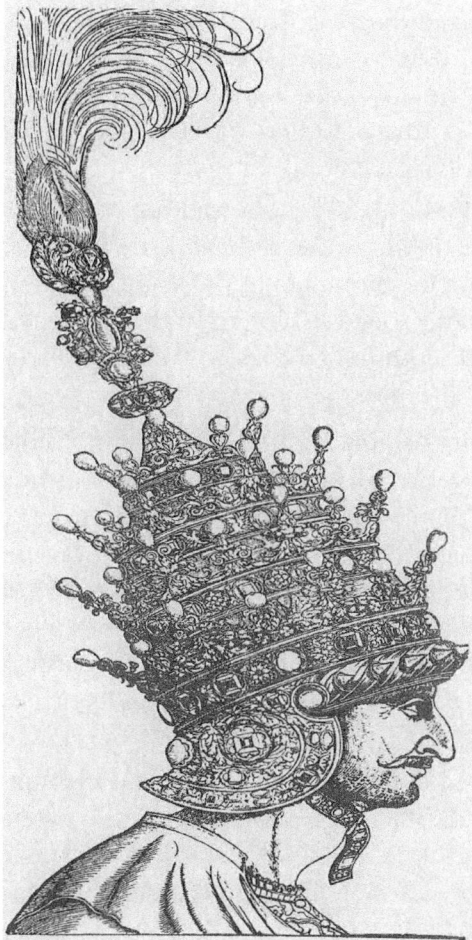

Suleiman's crown-helmet shown in a German wood engraving.

It was a strange object, part war helmet and part crown, with four tiers—one more than the pope's, which certainly conveyed a message to Western viewers. But Ottoman sultans did not wear crowns, so the Turks would not have understood its purpose, and it is likely the extravagant headgear was eventually melted down. It also focused many minds, not least that of Suleiman's treasurer, on whether Ibrahim was becoming too much of a spendthrift.

Ibrahim's thirteen years of power came to a sudden end in 1536. One possible cause was a quarrel with Suleiman's treasurer, or *defterdar*, Iskender Çelebi. The treasurer had fallen out with Ibrahim during the 1532 campaign against the Safavids: he criticized the vizier for extending the Iraqi campaign as far as Baghdad, at high cost. According to some sources, Çelebi was hanged when he endangered Suleiman's army by immobilizing it in enemy territory, against Ibrahim's advice. Other sources state that Ibrahim created a false pretext for his execution.

The story runs that Çelebi, having been informed of his impending execution, wrote a final letter to Suleiman, accusing Ibrahim of betraying the sultan to the shah. The word of a man who knows he is about to die is considered highly trustworthy—he has nothing to lose, nothing to gain—so Suleiman believed him. That was the end for Ibrahim.

Another story is that Hürrem was responsible. Ibrahim had supported Şehzade Mustafa, Mahidevran's son, as Suleiman's successor, which put him at odds with Hürrem, the mother of Suleiman's other sons. This, however, turns out to be a story that was not current at the time but was invented later. Since the Venetians were good inventors of conspiracy theories about the Ottoman sultans and their families, it is surprising that there is no contemporary rumor, and the story is most likely false.

What we do know is that Ibrahim had become increasingly arrogant. He had always been boastful, and his rapid rise may have gone to his head. Suleiman is reputed to have asked him which was the greater and more splendid festival: Ibrahim's marriage or the circumcision of the sultan's oldest sons. Ibrahim replied, "my marriage," though he explained to Suleiman in a flattering way that this was because his marriage had been graced by the sultan, whereas the sultan could not invite any guest of higher status than himself to his son's circumcision. That kind of wit is fun for a while, but eventually it begins to grate. Or, perhaps, Suleiman did not understand the joke.

Ibrahim did a lot of bragging to Westerners. For instance, he told Ferdinand's ambassadors, "It is I who govern this vast empire. What I do is done; I have all the power, all offices, all the rule. What I wish to give is given and cannot be taken away; what I do not give is not confirmed by any one. If ever the great sultan wishes to give, or has given anything, if I do not please it is not carried out. All is in my hands, peace, war, treasure. I do not say these things for no reason, but to give you courage to speak freely."[9]

It is quite likely he was saying this to get Ferdinand's ambassadors to commit themselves. In other words, he was expressing the fact that Suleiman had given him his full confidence. But if those words were reported to the sultan, he must have found them worrying.

(There is an interesting parallel here with the splendor-loving Cardinal Thomas Wolsey, Henry VIII's first minister, who had fallen from power just six years before Ibrahim. It was rumored that one reason Henry had turned against him was that Wolsey's palace at Hampton Court was more splendid than the king's palace at Whitehall. Wolsey's inability to negotiate an agreement with the Vatican for Henry's divorce from his first wife was also an issue.)

Ibrahim had also brought back statues from Buda and set them up in front of his palace in defiance of the Islamic injunction against making human images. This seems to have shocked many residents of Istanbul. There were rumors that he was a crypto-Christian, an infidel who had reneged on his Muslim faith. A satirical poet wrote that the world had seen "two Ibrahims, the one who destroyed idols and the one who set them up."[10] (Ibrahim is the Arabic name of the patriarch Abraham, who in both the Quran and the Jewish Midrash is said to have destroyed his father's idols.) Ibrahim had the poet sent around the city tied to a donkey before having him executed. Obviously, the taunt was not one he was prepared to tolerate, quite likely because it was dangerous.

In short, Ibrahim Pasha had become a worry and a liability to Suleiman. One night in March 1536, he dined with the sultan as usual and, after dinner, went to bed. He was strangled in his room by two of Suleiman's gardeners. (The Topkapi gardeners doubled as executioners, one of the Ottoman Empire's weirdest features.) Ibrahim had been *makbul*, the favorite; now he was Ibrahim

---

[9] *Jenkins, Hester Donaldson. Ibrahim Pasha: Grand Vizier of Suleiman the Magnificent (1911).*

[10] *Clot, André. Suleiman the Magnificent. Saqi Books. 2005.*

maktul, the executed.

But even in putting Ibrahim to death, Suleiman decided to go against tradition. Viziers were usually beheaded; lower officials might be hanged. But Ibrahim was strangled with a silken cord—a fate usually reserved for the royal family since it was forbidden to spill the blood of the sultan's kin. Yet again, where Suleiman's feelings were involved, he was prepared to break conventional rules.

But after Ibrahim's death, the grand vizier was completely obliterated. He was not given a *turbe*, or a marked grave; instead, he was buried in the courtyard of a dervish house, with only a tree to mark the place. Suleiman had killed someone he trusted and even loved, but having done so, he eradicated all trace of him. Perhaps he simply could not bear to know where Ibrahim was buried.

Ayas Mehmed Pasha became the next grand vizier and kept this position until his death (from natural causes) in 1539. He was succeeded by Lütfi Pasha, but when Lütfi's wife, Shah Sultan, a half-sister of Suleiman, accused the vizier of cruelty and asked for a divorce, he was sacked. Hadim Suleiman Pasha was then named as grand vizier in his place. In his turn, Hadim Suleiman was sacked, reputedly after bawling out his fourth vizier in front of the sultan.

It looked as if Suleiman was now committed to turning over his grand viziers every few years. None of them became his confidants. But Rustem Pasha, who took over for Hadim Suleiman Pasha in 1544, kept the position until his death in 1561 (apart from the two-year period of exile after the execution of Şehzade Mustafa).

Rustem, with his wife Mihrimah and mother-in-law Hürrem, created a strong political nucleus within the Topkapi Palace. But Rustem never enjoyed the intimate relationship that Parga Ibrahim had with Suleiman, though his shrewdness and thrifty nature helped him retain Suleiman's trust in a way the spendthrift Ibrahim had not been able to.

The execution of Pargali Ibrahim Pasha marked the beginning of a change in Suleiman and the nature of his rule. The sultan seems to have turned inward; he moved from military expansion toward the work of law and administration, creating justice and administrative systems that would stabilize the empire. Ibrahim's talents for display and military command were no longer indispensable; Suleiman was setting up a system that needed steady workers, not flashy young men in a hurry.

Suleiman may already have been starting to suffer from the gout that made his last years miserable; this would explain his withdrawal from active military campaigning.

But perhaps Suleiman was also lonely. A sultan was not allowed a personal life; he had broken the rules for Ibrahim, but his friendship had been destroyed. His guilt may have pushed him toward more serious spiritual pursuits. Certainly, he never again confided in a member of his own sex the way he had in Ibrahim; for the rest of his reign, his advisers were women—his wife Hűrrem and his daughter Mihrimah.

Ibrahim's career was like a meteor: shining splendidly and then falling to earth. Everything he touched turned to gold for thirteen years, and then he fell.

But perhaps we should be asking whether Ibrahim was really a success in everything he touched. That is the story from the official chronicler, Celâlzâde Mustafa. But Celâlzâde was as much a propagandist for the sultan as a historian. He may have written up Ibrahim's talents and achievements to make Suleiman's choice of vizier look better.

There is another very different view of Ibrahim Pasha: that he was over-promoted, spoiled, and devoid of talent and that he mercilessly exploited Suleiman's affection for him. A report sent back to Venice by a Venetian spy in 1534 accused Ibrahim of neglecting the army and navy, sidelining capable men, and weakening the empire. As happens so often in corporate life and politics, a smart young man had upset the older, more conservative management, who considered him over-promoted. Perhaps he was.

Ibrahim Pasha's story sums up the splendor and the danger of Ottoman court life. But it is worth noting that while being grand vizier to Suleiman was dangerous, Suleiman's father Selim had a much worse record. He went through six grand viziers in his eight-year reign, executing three of them. Apparently, viziers had a habit of never going from their homes to Topkapi Palace without putting a copy of their will in their pocket, and a popular curse of the time was "May you be a vizier of Selim's!" Being a vizier of Suleiman's was a much lower risk.

Chapter 10: Death and Legacy

Suleiman was victorious even in death. As he died in his tent near Szigetvár, his army was preparing for the next day's conquest. He had lived a long life, and it had been a lifetime of high achievement.

But this was a dangerous moment for the Ottoman Empire, even though Suleiman had only one son left to inherit. Selim was currently in Anatolia, far to the east. If the news got to Istanbul before Selim did, there would be a power vacuum in the capital as well as in the army. Who might take advantage? The Persians, for instance, might take the opportunity to invade a weakened empire. If Maximilian knew the Ottoman army was leaderless, he would be able to decimate it.

So, Sokollu Mehmed Pasha decided to keep the sultan's death a secret. He is said to have executed all witnesses to Suleiman's death, including his doctor; he then explained the sultan's non-appearance to the army by saying he was too ill to perform his duties. Since everyone knew that Suleiman often suffered terribly from his gout, this was an acceptable excuse—for a while, anyway. Suleiman was embalmed; his heart was buried at Szigetvár together with his other organs. Later, Selim built a mausoleum and shrine on the site, and this became a site of pilgrimage for local Muslims until it was eventually destroyed by the Austrians.

Tipped off by the loyal Sokollu Mehmed Pasha, Şehzade Selim quickly made his way back from Anatolia. It was only 48 days after Suleiman's death, however, that the news of Selim's accession could be announced ceremonially. In this way, the security of the succession was assured.

It is interesting to ponder whether Suleiman would be remembered in the same way had he died leaving Bayezid and Selim to battle things out. The empire might well have fractured again. That could easily have caused a decade of civil war, leaving the Ottomans weak and vulnerable not only to attack from the West and from Persia but also to the rebellion of provinces such as Egypt and Iraq. As it was, he left a strong empire and an uncontested succession, together with a civil and military administration strong enough to survive several sultans who were at best lackluster and at worst completely mad.

Suleiman had definitely made changes in the way the sultan lived, particularly in the position of the haseki sultan. Selim—"the Blond" or "the Drunk" depending on the historian—like his father, adopted a modified style of monogamy. He made his preferred concubine, Nurbanu Sultan, his legal wife and brought her to live with him in the Topkapi Palace, just as Suleiman had done with Hürrem. In fact, when Nurbanu's son Murad III succeeded to the throne, Nurbanu became immensely powerful as valide sultan. Murad, in turn, chose a single consort, Safiye Sultan. Though he later took other concubines and had many children by them, Safiye had only one challenger for Murad's affections—his mother, Nurbanu. In her turn, Safiye became valide sultan to her son with Murad, Mehmed III.

There was a certain amount of continuity from Suleiman's reign going into Selim's. The loyal Sokollu Mehmed Pasha remained grand vizier, and Suleiman's daughter Mihrimah continued to advise her brother, as well as lend him money (probably to pay the Janissaries on his accession).

Later, the valide sultans also helped provide continuity between one reign and the next. The valide sultans, in fact, were responsible for what has sometimes been called a "sultanate of women" from Hürrem's time to the end of the seventeenth century. While they have traditionally been seen as enfeebling the empire, they also helped ensure smooth transitions of power and the continuity of policy. For instance, when the "mad" Ibrahim was dethroned, his mother, Kösem Sultan, did not retire to the Old Palace, as was tradition, but stayed as elder or "greater" valide sultan (*büyük* valide sultan) to her grandson Mehmed, since Mehmed's mother Turhan Sultan was young and inexperienced.

Suleiman vastly increased the expanse of the Ottoman Empire, and after his death, it continued to expand. In 1571, the Ottomans took Cyprus from Venice; Morocco, Mogadishu, and all of Yemen were also added to the Ottoman world. But unlike Suleiman, a veteran campaigner right up to his death, his successors Selim II and Murad III never left Istanbul once they became sultans. The court became more distant from the empire. At the same time, the devshirme system started to show its age; Turkish families resented being marginalized from positions of power, and by the 1650s, the system was on its way out.

Even so, the Ottoman Empire continued to prosper in the century after Suleiman's death. Perhaps most importantly, Suleiman had not only extended the borders of the empire but also given Turkey a strong influence in Europe, where it could help determine the balance of power. Turkey now had to be considered in European politics; monarchs such as Elizabeth I of England corresponded with and sent embassies to the sultan. In 1867, Queen Victoria received Sultan Abdülaziz on a state visit to London and invested him with the Order of the Garter on board the royal yacht. In fact, it was the West that, awed by the splendor and power of Suleiman, gave him the name "Suleiman the Magnificent." For Turks, he is still "the Lawgiver," though the recent Turkish TV series *Magnificent Century* has popularized his other title.

But while the title "magnificent" was bestowed by his enemies, it is true that the Ottomans saw Suleiman's reign as a golden age. In fact, nostalgia for Suleiman's magnificence was probably one of the factors that most handicapped the later Ottoman sultans; they knew they could never compete with the past, and the Ottoman Empire as a whole began to look back and inward.

Does Suleiman really deserve the immense respect he is given? After all, he started with huge advantages: no brothers to fight for the throne, the conquests made by his father Selim, and the existing Ottoman advantage in artillery together with the beginnings of a navy. The whole bureaucracy of the Ottoman state, the devshirme system, and the administration of the different provinces had already been set up. He inherited a powerful machine, which he simply needed to learn to use.

A lesser man, though, might not have been able to maintain this empire, let alone expand it. Within the first two years of his reign, he had made two spectacular conquests—Rhodes and Belgrade. Even with all his advantages, his daring and his achievement were notable.

Suleiman has also been criticized for over-reliance on his two favorites—first Ibrahim Pasha, then Hűrrem. But his early successes were all achieved with Ibrahim, including the reintegration of Egypt, in which Ibrahim was working without his sultan's daily presence. Suleiman appears to have chosen wisely. As for Hűrrem, she has been widely blamed for the death of Ibrahim, the execution of Mustafa, and the eventual fall of the Ottoman Empire, becoming a stereotype of the scheming queen. As a woman of the harem, she would have had no chance to defend herself against such accusations. In any case, the Ottoman dynastic system was set up on exactly the idea that a woman would do almost anything to ensure her son's succession to the throne. The only difference was that, unlike previous concubines who were expected to retire from the sultan's bed once they had borne him a single son, Hűrrem stayed and had what would now be considered a normal family with him.

In fact, Suleiman does not appear to have made any grave strategic mistakes through being given bad advice by either Ibrahim or Hűrrem. He may have broken the rules to allow himself intimacy with his favorites, but given the stresses of a sultan's existence, can we blame him?

He had the clear sight to recognize the advances made by his predecessors and to understand the need for continued investment in firepower and in the navy. In law, too, his codification of the Ottoman laws can be seen as recognizing his predecessors' work while aiming to give it a structure and consistency it did not then possess.

Suleiman also knew how to use diplomacy on a grand scale. He had the astuteness and the intelligence network to know what was happening to the balance of power in Europe and put that knowledge to good use.

His age was an age of great monarchs. He was contemporary with Henry VIII of England, Francois I of France, Charles V the Holy Roman Emperor, and Ivan the Terrible of Russia; his reign overlapped at one end with that of Shah Ismail of Persia and at the other with the rule of the great Emperor Akbar of India. Suleiman held his own in this company.

However, he never achieved the definitive success he was looking for on either the eastern or western borders of his empire. For instance, he was never able to press home his advantage in the Mediterranean and failed twice to conquer Vienna. Nor did he ever manage to subdue Iran. (His father had added Egypt to the empire; perhaps he dreamed of adding Iran as a way of equaling his father's achievement.)

In fact, if Suleiman had attacked India early in his reign, with his advantages in artillery as well as his ability to bring reinforcements by sea, he may have been able to create an even more extensive empire. India at the time was in disarray, with smaller states continuing to fight against Mughal domination. By the time Akbar acceded to his grandfather Babur's throne, Suleiman had lost his chance.

Perhaps Suleiman was simply too aware of the danger of extending his lines of supply too far. In any case, taking Buda at one end of his empire and Baghdad at the other could hardly be described as failure. He successfully retained the unity of the empire his father had left him while expanding its economy and creating a legal code that could support the increasing modernization of the Ottoman world.

Many historical figures are known for their conquests. But there is another aspect to Suleiman: he was both an investor in infrastructure and a lover and patron of the arts. The two went together, as Sinan's career shows: building robust bridges and useful khans was as much a part of his job as creating the mosques that were his masterpieces. In particular, Suleiman transformed the landscape of Istanbul.

Everywhere in Istanbul are buildings of his time. The Mihrimah Sultan Mosque dominates the shore at Üsküdar; Suleiman's own mosque dominates the third hill of the city; the mosque he built for his father Selim overlooks the Golden Horn. *Hammams* and smaller mosques, soup kitchens, hospitals, and hans funded by members of his family and administration are shoehorned into every corner of the city.

Perhaps the best way of judging Suleiman, though, is to look at the men who surrounded him: Ibrahim Pasha, Sokollu Mehmet Pasha, Barbarossa, Sinan, Piri Reis. He filled his administration, his navy, and his army with men of talent, knowing that he needed greatness in his servants as well as magnificence in his personality. Perhaps that is the true measure of his greatness.

Conclusion

Suleiman was born into a world that was changing dramatically in both the East and West. In the West, Protestantism was beginning to make an impact, the discovery of the New World had just been made, and economies were slowly developing from feudal and agricultural to modern and commercial. In the East, three empires—the Ottoman, Persian, and Indian—were rising, and Portuguese exploration had brought India and the Far East closer to Europe.

He was equal to the challenges of his time. In his first years, he was almost perpetually on the move, fighting to secure and expand the frontiers of his state and ensure the loyalty of recently-acquired provinces such as Egypt and Syria. Later, as he grew older and was affected by gout, he left more to his sons and pashas; even so, in his seventies, he did not hesitate to set out once more against the Habsburgs.

Suleiman was not some unlettered, savage tyrant like Genghis Khan or Timur. He was capable of hard decisions, but he appears to have ruled in the way he intended on his accession: with justice and for the benefit of his people. It may seem strange to commend a man responsible for the deaths of his best friend and two of his sons as merciful, but seen in the context of the Ottoman Empire (and particularly of his father Selim), he was one of the least bloodthirsty sultans.

In particular, he issued a *ferman* denouncing blood libels against the Jews in 1553. (The idea is said to have come from his physician,

Moses Hamon, an emigrant from Spain, which had expelled the Jews in 1492.) It was mainly Christians who accused Jews of killing and eating Christian children in a parody of the Eucharist, so this was not a common accusation within the Ottoman Empire. But, as he expanded his realm to the west, Suleiman decided it was important to protect his Jewish subjects.

That did not translate into mercy for his enemies. Christians were tolerated in the empire, even as vassal rulers, but he was ruthless toward Christian opponents, as were his men. One story tells how Mustafa Pasha had beheaded the defenders of Fort Saint Elmo at Malta and sent their bodies across the harbor to the Grand Master of the Knights. He, in turn, had all his Turkish prisoners beheaded and fired their heads as cannonballs at the Ottomans. Suleiman is also said to have had all the prisoners taken at Mohacs executed the day after. No doubt some of these stories were over-dramatized—the numbers of combatants, for instance, are often exaggerated—but there is no doubt that atrocities were committed on both sides.

Even so, Suleiman took good care of the subjects living under his rule. It is not the sign of a tyrant to have the law read out in public so that people know their rights or to create a system of checks and balances to prevent corrupt and oppressive rule by provincial governors.

Suleiman transformed the Ottoman Empire, and he transformed Istanbul. The city must have been a paradise compared to many European capitals. There were public schools and hospitals, soup kitchens for the indigent, and well-policed consumer markets with clear rules on quality and price. The quality of the infrastructure was excellent, without even considering that many of these buildings were masterpieces of architecture.

But in some ways, Suleiman's life was a tragedy. He served the Ottoman state well, but he had lost his favorite son Mehmed, his much-loved friend Ibrahim, and, in his last years, his beloved wife. He was always fighting on one front or another, always weighing his pashas' loyalties, always working. A sultan's life was a lonely one, and perhaps he always had his grandfather's fate at the back of his mind: would he, in turn, be betrayed by one of his sons?

Look at portraits of him with his intense eyes and nose like an eagle's beak, and you will begin to wonder whether he was ever truly content. He managed to find some moments of happiness, at least, with Hűrrem, to whom he wrote poetry:

"My throne, my treasury, my love, my moonlight,

My best friend, my confidant, my very being, my Sultan, my only love,

most beautiful of all the beauties.

My woman of the beautiful air, my slant-browed love, with eyes full of mischief,

I will always sing your praise.

I, Muhibbi, tormented lover, my eyes full of tears—I am happy."

Summary of Dates

1494	Birth of Suleiman in Trabzon
1520	Accession as sultan
1521	Taking of Belgrade
1522	Siege of Rhodes
1523	Pargali Ibrahim Pasha becomes grand vizier
1526	Battle of Mohacs
1529	First siege of Vienna
1532	Taking of Kőszeg
1534	Baghdad taken
1534	Marriage with Hűrrem Sultan
1536	Murder of Pargali Ibrahim Pasha

1537	Attempt on Corfu unsuccessful
1538	Invasion of Moldavia, annexation of Bessarabia
1541	Siege of Buda: Hungary annexed
1543	Capture of Székesfehérvár, Siklos, and Szeged
1543	Death of Şehzade Mehmed
1548	Second Persian campaign
1551	Capture of Tripoli
1553	Third Persian campaign
1553	Execution of Şehzade Mustafa: death of Şehzade Cihangir
1555	Peace of Amasya signed with Safavids
1558	Death of Hűrrem Sultan
1559	Battle of Konya: Selim defeats Bayezid
1561	Execution of Şehzade Bayezid
1565	Siege of Malta
1566	Siege of Szigetvár: Death of Suleiman

Glossary

Bey	Governor of a district or province
Beylerbey	"Bey of beys," that is, commander-in-chief
devshirme	"collecting": Christian children taken for training in the palace schools and forming most of the administration and army
Enderun	"Interior," the inner court of the Topkapi Palace, also used for the private staff of the sultan
Enderun School	The palace school for gifted devshirme and male members of the royal family
Fetva	A ruling on religious law (from Arabic *fatwa*)
Firman or ferman	An edict issued by a sultan
Hammam	Turkish baths

Han	An inn for travelers
Harem	The "private" parts of the palace, where the sultan lived with his concubines, mother, daughters, and non-adult sons
Haseki sultan	Chief consort of an Ottoman sultan, a title first used for Hűrrem Sultan
Imaret	Soup kitchen
Janissary	"recruits" (Turkish *yeniçeri*): infantry troops recruited from devshirme children
Kadi or Qadi	A religious judge
Kanun	The body of secular law issued by the sultan (i.e., not sharia law)
Pasha	Title given to high-ranking officials
Rumelia	"Rome": the western or European lands of the empire
Sanjak (Turkish spelling *sancak*)	"Banner," used to define a provincial district. A şehzade would be sent to govern a sanjak as part of his training.
şehzade	Prince (son of a sultan)
sultan	Ruler of the Ottomans: also used as an honorific prefix (for males of the royal family) or suffix (for females)

Tughra	The calligraphic signature of the sultan, as used on legal and state documents
Turbe	Mausoleum
Valide sultan	The queen mother: mother of a reigning sultan
Vizier	A high official, usually given the title pasha
Voivode	Slavic "warlord"; in the Balkans, a military leader or duke

Here's another book by Enthralling History that you might like

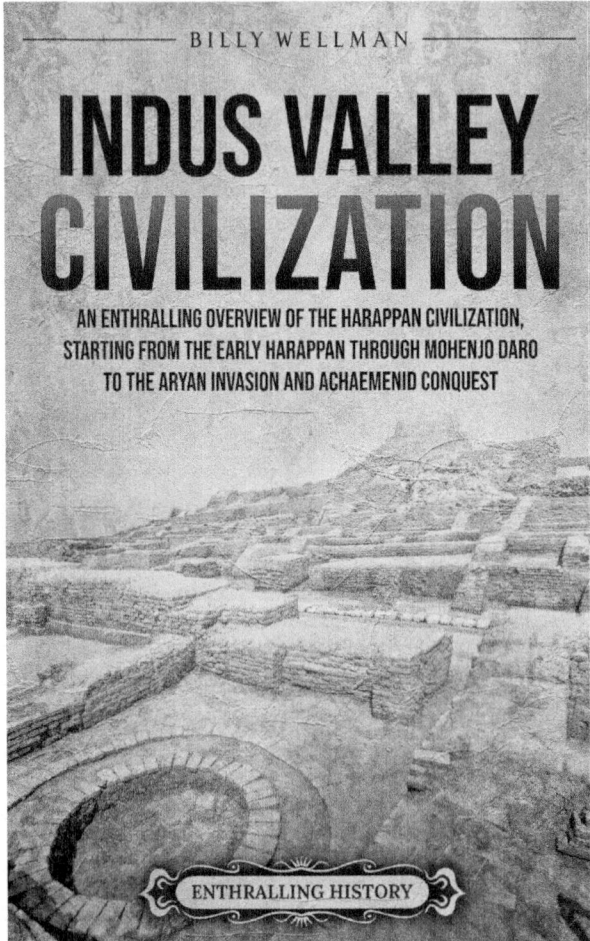

BILLY WELLMAN

INDUS VALLEY CIVILIZATION

AN ENTHRALLING OVERVIEW OF THE HARAPPAN CIVILIZATION, STARTING FROM THE EARLY HARAPPAN THROUGH MOHENJO DARO TO THE ARYAN INVASION AND ACHAEMENID CONQUEST

ENTHRALLING HISTORY

Free limited time bonus

Stop for a moment. We have a free bonus set up for you. The problem is this: we forget 90% of everything that we read after 7 days. Crazy fact, right? Here's the solution: we've created a printable, 1-page pdf summary for this book that you're reading now. All you have to do to get your free pdf summary is to go to the following website:

https://livetolearn.lpages.co/enthrallinghistory/

Once you do, it will be intuitive. Enjoy, and thank you!

We forget 90% of everything that we've read in 7 days...

Get the free printable pdf summary of the book you've read AND much, much more... shhhh...

Enter Your Most Frequently Used Email to Get Started

DOWNLOAD FREE PDF SUMMARY

© Enthralling History

Sources

1. Bloxham, D. (2003). "The Armenian Genocide of 1915-1916: Cumulative Radicalization and the Development of a Destruction Policy." Past & Present, 181, 141–191. http://www.jstor.org/stable/3600788.

2. Brown, P. M. (1924). "From Sevres to Lausanne." The American Journal of International Law, 18(1), 113–116. https://doi.org/10.2307/2189228.

3. Clot, André. (2012). *Suleiman the Magnificent.* Saqi. Retrieved October 10, 2022.

4. Der Matossian, B. (2014). *Shattered Dreams of Revolution: From Liberty to Violence in the Late Ottoman Empire.* Stanford University Press. Retrieved October 10, 2022.

5. Guilmartin, J. F. (1988). "Ideology and Conflict: The Wars of the Ottoman Empire, 1453-1606." The Journal of Interdisciplinary History, 18(4), 721–747. https://doi.org/10.2307/204822

6. Harris, J. (2010). *The End of Byzantium.* Yale University Press. https://doi.org/10.12987/9780300169669.

7. Imber, C. (2002). *The Ottoman Empire, 1300-1650: The Structure of Power.* Palgrave Macmillan.

8. Kedourie, E. (1968). "The End of the Ottoman Empire." Journal of Contemporary History, 3(4), 19–28. http://www.jstor.org/stable/259848.

9. Kia, M. (2008). *The Ottoman Empire* (Ser. Greenwood Guides to Historic Events, 1500-1900). Greenwood Press. Retrieved October 10, 2022.

10. Quataert, D. (2005). *The Ottoman Empire, 1700-1922* (2nd ed., Ser. New approaches to European History). Cambridge University Press.

11. ŞAHİN, K. (2017). "The Ottoman Empire in the Long Sixteenth Century." Renaissance Quarterly, 70(1), 220–234. https://www.jstor.org/stable/26560197.

12. Shaw, S. Jay and Yapp, Malcolm Edward (2022, August 23). "Ottoman Empire." Encyclopedia Britannica. https://www.britannica.com/place/Ottoman-Empire.

13. "The Ottoman Empire in the Eighteenth Century." (1992). Turkish Studies Association Bulletin, 16(2), 179–216. http://www.jstor.org/stable/43385332.

14. Wajih Kawtharani. (2018). "The Ottoman Tanzimat and the Constitution." AlMuntaqa, 1(1), 51–65. https://doi.org/10.31430/almuntaqa.1.1.0051.

15. Atil, Esin. *The Age of Sultan Suleyman the Magnificent.* National Gallery of Art, Washington. 1987.

16. Bradford, Ernle (1968). *The Sultan's Admiral: The Life of Barbarossa. New York: Harcourt, Brace & World; London: Hodder & Stoughton 1969.*

17. Barber, Noel (1976). *Lords of the Golden Horn: From Suleiman the Magnificent to Kamal Ataturk. London: Pan Books. ISBN.*

18. Black, Jeremy (ed). *The Seventy Great Battles of All Time. Thames & Hudson, 2005.*

19. Clot, André. *Suleiman the Magnificent. Saqi Books. 2005.*

20. El-Moghazi, Honey. *"The Innovations in the Ottoman Legal Administration: The 16th Century between Theory and Practice." American University in Cairo, 2018.*

21. Finkel, Caroline (2005). *Osman's Dream: The Story of the Ottoman Empire, 1300–1923. New York: Basic Books. ISBN.*

22. Fisher, Alan (1993). *"The Life and Family of Süleymân I." In İnalcık, Halil; Kafadar, Cemal (eds.). Süleymân The Second [i.e., the First] and His Time. Istanbul: Isis Press.*

23. Gilles, Pierre. *The Antiquities of Constantinople, translated by John Ball. London 1729.*

24. Halman, S. Talat. *Poems by Suleyman the Magnificent under the Pseudonym Muhibbi. Millenium. 2007.*

25. Jenkins, Hester Donaldson. *Ibrahim Pasha: Grand Vizier of Suleiman the Magnificent (1911).*

26. Lamb, Harold. *Suleiman the Magnificent: Sultan of the East* (1951).

27. Peirce, Leslie. Imperial Harem: *Women and Sovereignty in the Ottoman Empire.* Oxford University Press. 1993.

28. Şahin, Kaya (2013). *Empire and Power in the Reign of Süleyman: Narrating the Sixteenth-Century Ottoman World.* Cambridge University Press. ISBN.

29. Sakaoğlu, Necdet. *Famous Ottoman Women.* 2007.

30. Stratton, Arthur. *Sinan: The Biography of One of the World's Greatest Architects and a Portrait of the Golden Age of the Ottoman Empire.* Scribner, 1971.

31. Tucker, Spencer. *Battles That Changed History: An Encyclopedia of World Conflict.* 2010.

Printed in Great Britain
by Amazon